A CRITIQUE OF MUSICOLOGY

Clarifying the Scope, Limits, and Purposes of Musicology

John A. Kimmey, Jr.

A CRITIQUE OF MUSICOLOGY
Clarifying the Scope, Limits, and Purposes of Musicology

John A. Kimmey, Jr.

Studies in the History and Interpretation of Music
Volume 12

The Edwin Mellen Press
Lewiston/Queenston
Lampeter

Library of Congress Cataloging-in-Publication Data

Kimmey, John A.
   A critique of musicology : clarifying the scope, limits, and
purposes of musicology / John A. Kimmey, Jr.
     p. cm. -- (Studies in the history and interpretation of music
; v. 12)
     Bibliography: p.
     Includes index.
     ISBN 0-88946-437-5
     1. Musicology. I. Title. II. Series.
ML3797.K55 1988
780'.1--dc19   88-9355
                                                  CIP
                                                 MN

This is volume 12 in the continuing series
Studies in History & Interpretation of Music
Volume 12 ISBN 0-88946-437-5
SHIM Series ISBN 0-88946-426—X

The Edwin Mellen Press
Box 450   Box 67
Lewiston, New York   Queenston, Ontario
USA 14092   L0S 1L0 CANADA
Mellen House
Lampeter, Dyfed, Wales
UNITED KINGDOM SA48 7DY

Printed in the United States of America

to the memory of
KENNETH G. WHITE
and
ELIZABETH BRETT KIMMEY

TABLE OF CONTENTS

ACKNOWLEDGEMENTS

The nature of space is such that all of those individuals who aided and abetted in the production of this work cannot be mentioned at once. Appearing first, or last, on the list of acknowledgments does not imply, on my part, priority or lack of priority in my estimation of the aid received on this project.

For reading the manuscript and the many valuable suggestions, thanks go to Professor Marilyn Gombosi, Drs. Russell Dancy, Eugene F. Kaelin and David Gruender.

For the many hours of helpful conversation and dialogue on a multitude of musicological topics I must thank Dr. R. Fred Kern, John W. Terrell and James B. Parsons.

A special note of thanks goes to Morris Martin, music librarian at North Texas State University, for giving me absolute freedom in his library, including the forbidden "Locked Case."

Proofreading, the translation of Guido Adler's article and the music examples would have been impossible without David Lively's eagle eye and steady hand.

Thanks, also, must go to Kathy Copeland for typing and editing the final copy--her editorial powers are

renowned.   However, I must take credit (blame) for all
discrepancies remaining in the text.

Last, but by no means least, many thanks to
Elizabeth B. Kimmey for the mental, spiritual and
financial help necessary for the completion of this
project.

LIST OF ILLUSTRATIONS

PREFACE

A few words are in order before we begin this
critique of musicology. The time-period covered in
the retrospective, Pythagoras to the end of the 19th
century, is enormous; and the number of individuals who
have written about music in that time frame are legion.
The inclusion criteria for the retrospective are twofold: consider those writers who have made lasting and
innovative contributions to the study of music, this
means those writers who are "remembered" in histories of
the discipline; and everywhere delete redundancy using
Ockham's razor, i.e., <u>entia</u> <u>non</u> <u>sunt</u> <u>multiplicanda</u>
<u>praeter</u> <u>necessitatem</u>--entities are not to be multiplied
beyond need. The critique itself, then, is drawn from
the data collected in the retrospective and those 20th-
century writers who have contributed to each field
within musicology. This limitation is in accordance
with phenomeno-logical methods which demand scientific
rigor in that <u>all</u> descriptions and conclusions must
come from the data collected of observed phenomena.

Of course, this is not the only critique of
musicology possible because another set of originary
phenomena, i.e., another collection of writers on music,
could be chosen as the ground of the study. Also,
musicology itself is not a closed discipline, it is an
unfinished project undergoing constant change. Any
attempt, under these circumstances, to write <u>THE</u> critique
of musicology would not only be futile but arrogant.

All those whose lives are spent
searching for truth are well aware
that the glimpses they catch of it
are necessarily fleeting, glittering
for an instant only to make way for
new and still more dazzling
insights. The scholar's work, in
marked contrast to that of the
artist, is inevitably provisional.
He knows this and rejoices in it,
for the rapid obsolescence of his
books is the very proof of the
progress of scholarship.

--Henri Pirenne

*...it is much easier to accept standards that
are prepared for you. Beware of the dead.*

--Rupert Brooke, <u>Democracy & the Arts</u>

CHAPTER I

INTRODUCTION: THE PROBLEM

§ 1. <u>Presentation of the problem through a
definition of terms</u>

The fundamental objective of this work is to
describe and clarify the scope, limits and purposes of
musicology, both historical and systematic, as the science of musical phenomena. Let us unpack this statement. The title of the work indicates that it is conceived as a critique. It is a critique in the Kantian
mode, and following Kant's formulation in the preface to
the first edition to his <u>Critique of Pure Reason</u>, this
critique will "decide as to the possibility or impossi-
bility of ⟨musicology⟩ in general, and determine its
sources, its extent, and its limits--all in accordance
with principles."[1] Again, in the preface to the second
edition of the same work Kant explains the rôle of a
critique <u>vis-à-vis</u> its subject matter.

It is a treatise on the method, not a system
of the science itself. But at the same time
it marks out the whole plan of the science,
both as regards its entire internal
structure.[2]

Pursuant to Kant's explanation, this critique concerns
itself with the methods of musicology, and is not a
system of musicology itself. The complete musicological
project is clarified and described "both as regards its
limits and . . . its entire internal structure." In
order to start such a critique, the many and varied
concepts and definitions of musicology that have been
used by writers on music must be delineated.

These definitions are legion. Even though in some
musicological circles any attempt to define the term is
considered utter folly, we must set forth at least some
of them in order to grasp the methods that the discipline uses. It is from these terminological concepts
that our investigation must start. These definitions
range from the most general, i.e., the scholarly study
of music, and includes every conceivable discussion of
musical topics; to a presentation of musicology as a
science; the whole body of systematized knowledge about
music through the application of scientific method, and
all the sciences which deal with the production,
appearance and application of the physical phenomenon
called sound. Also, musicology has been defined
negatively: it is everything that is not in the domain
of applied music. In other words, musicology has
nothing to do with the actual performance of music.
University curricula reflect this attitude; one either

studies musicology, music theory OR performance on some
instrument, i.e., applied music. Musicology has also
been styled as an activity; people "do" musicology.
They engage in the activity of musical studies. On the
other hand, it can be seen as an area of knowledge that
exists regardless of that activity. Under this rubric
musicology is a systematized and ordered area of
knowledge about music. Many maps of musical knowledge
demonstrate this regional attitude towards musicology.
Such diverse writers as Aristides Quintilianus, J. N.
Forkel[3] and Guido Adler have supplied us with such maps.
The humanistic sciences of the 20th century have caused
some musicologists to shift the traditional core of
musical studies, i.e., music, to Man the musician as the
core. Music, in this guise, is seen as a cultural
phenomenon to be studied as a human activity and not as
a unique or isolated phenomenon. Music is no longer
fixed in a "composition," to be studied as an autonomous
object, but becomes part of the flux of human activity.
The shift, then, is from an historical study to a
sociological-anthropological one.

Musicology itself is traditionally divided between
historical studies and systematics, i.e., music theory,
aesthetics, etc.[4] The roots and reasons behind this
duality in the nature of musicology are thoroughly
explored in the retrospective. The rationale behind
Guido Adler's[5] bifurcation rests on two points: tradition, going back to Aristides Quintilianus; and the
nature of the subject matter, music, as theory and as
practice. Once these notions behind the duality have
been thematized they can be used as a tool in the

critical study both descriptively and in delineating the
future domain of musicology.

In doing a critique one must distinguish between
the science itself and its methods, as Kant has pointed
out. In the case of musicology we can distinguish
between applied musicology and the methods that the
definitions and attitudes mentioned above imply. These
methods can roughly be divided between those that belong
to the Naturwissenschaften and the Geisteswissenschaften
plus a bevy of Hilfswissenschaften, all of which will be
thematized in the critique. Applied musicology is the
application of methods, scientific or humanistic, to the
phenomenon of music. This distinction implies that
these methods can be separated from musicology per se
and in turn become the object of scrutiny. When in this
modality, we are doing metamusicology. If musicology is
seen as an area of knowledge, there are "objects" in
that field, e.g., music as physical, psychological,
aesthetic and cultural phenomena, which, in turn, are
investigated. This investigation is the application of
methods to produce the science of musical phenomena:
musicology. To disengage these methods and view them as
an object for investigation is to move into the realm of
metamusicology. The change in focus from musicology to
metamusicology is a change from an objective focus (the
field of musical phenomena) to a subjective one (the
tools and methods used by musicologists to investigate
the musical field). Musicology proper is objective in
that it uses a variety of methods to study the musical
given, the given being "outside" the methods used to
thematize them. When the musicologist turns toward the

methods used, he makes a subjective turn. He will not
consider exploring the possibilities for undertaking
musicological thinking. Edmund Husserl speaks to this
very focal change in his Formal and Transcendental
Logic:

> It may be that shifts to the subjective focus
> are occasionally helpful or even necessary to
> what he truly has in view, namely the theory
> of his practice; as in other far-seeing
> actions, so in theoretical actions the need
> may arise to deliberate reflectively and ask,
> "What method shall I try now? What premises
> can serve me?"[6]

§ 2. Phenomenology as supplying the sought-for critique

The particular phenomenon that is to be critically
scrutinized is musicology: that is our field of
investigation. The field will be approached without
preconceptions as to what musicology should be, but only
as it has been and is practiced by musicologists. The
given musicological field will be described as a unique
discipline and compared to other fields using similar
methods, e.g., anthropology, sociology, etc. in order to
help delineate musicological parameters. This comparison is necessary because musicology uses a variety of
auxiliary sciences as part of its methods.

What constitutes such phenomenological description?
Description is a classification of phenomena. Since

musicologists have already developed a classification
schema for the discipline, the task of a phenomenological description will be to locate the methods used in
devising that system of classes. J. S. Mill, in his A
System of Logic, points out "to describe is to affirm a
connection between it (an individual thing) and every
other thing which is either denoted or connoted by any
of the terms used."[7] All of the connections between
musicology as a class and the subclasses within the
field, e.g., music theory, iconography, performance
practice, etc., will be clarified and investigated. As
such the description will be genetic, going to the
foundations, and will be selective, not exhaustive of
all the intricate interrelationships between the strata
within the field. As nonexhaustive, the description is
meant to obtain and thematize guidelines to the phenomena themselves. This is so because musicology is not
a fixed phenomenon, it is in constant growth and change.
All any phenomenological description can hope to do is
define the parameters within which that flux occurs and
still be called "musicology." By the same token, the
question of the regional concept of musicology must be
criticized. For some the whole fabric of musicology as
an area of knowledge capable of schematization is moot.

Out of these descriptions of the field will emerge
the eidetic structure of musicology. The essential
characteristics of the discipline will become manifest
as the connections between particular parts of musicology are thematized. From these thematized particulars a
general type can be projected. When all the groups of
the musicological phenomenon are laid out for the
intuiting gaze of the phenomenologist, the core around

which they cluster will give insights into the nature of
those core ideas or essences. What happens is that the
structural affinities between particulars will "naturally" pull them to the ground of their similarities,
and this ground is the essence or eidetic structure.

Once the eidetic structure of musicology has been
gained, we are fast on our way to understanding the
essential relationships within the field, and to
defining the parameters of that field. To understand or
apprehend essential relationships the phenomenologist
uses a technique called "free imaginative variation."
The question to be asked is this: Could musicology
exist that does not have the eidetic structure obtained
in essential analysis? In order to answer that question
those essential components are freely varied in the
imagination either by leaving out some of them or
replacing them with others; or by varying the combinations of essences. In following such a procedure the
limits and scope of the essential characteristics of
musicology will be discovered. It is also possible that
free imaginative variation will show that what was
thought to be essential is indeed nonessential.

So far, in our discussion of how phenomenological
methods will be used in this investigation, modality has
not been mentioned. To the mode of appearance of musicology we must now turn. That musicology is not an
object in the sense that rocks, trees and cats are
objects is a trivial observation. But it must be stated
from the outset that musicology is not a natural phenomenon in the mode "extended thing in space." Musicology is a cultural, human-created phenomenon and thus

its modality is psychical not physical. The critique
will clarify this psychical mode.

Musicology, as a human activity, has an historical
manifestation, and it is to that historical aspect that
we must turn in order to effect our critical observations.

§ 3. Rôle of the retrospective in thematizing
sedimented ideas, concepts, methods, etc.

Edmund Husserl, in § 15 of his book Die Krisis
der europäischen Wissenschaften und die transzendentale
Phänomenologie, gives us an entrance into the use of
historical material for phenomenological investigations.
The musicological retrospective will be an inquiry back
into the writings of those Greek proto-musicologists
who established the teleology of musicology as we know
it today, i.e., divided between historical and systematic aspects. This matrix of causes and goals forms
the bedrock of sedimented thought upon which all subsequent musical thought has been built. A thorough
chronological-historical investigation will be done of
representative writers on music in order to clarify
their relationships to this primordial matrix. As these
relationships come to light the goals and purposes of
musicology will become manifest. The many classification schemata and methodologies will be seen to be
endless variations on an Hellenic theme. So, to paraphrase the Krisis, "our task is to make comprehensible
the teleology in the historical becoming of musicology
. . . we are attempting to elicit and understand the

unity running through all musicological projects that
oppose one another and work together in their changing
forms." Elucidation of this unity, via historical
retrospective, will give us essential insight which can
be used as a tool for a critical understanding of
musicology.

§ 4. Summary of aims

The final goal of this project is to criticize
musicology phenomenologically. To that end we will
search for the parameters of musicology and describe
them phenomenologically. Phenomenology will be used as
a tool to obtain descriptive and essential data which
will be used in doing the critique. The fundamental
methodology of our investigation is not only phenomenological but also historical. A general survey of the
progress of musicological thinking, from Pythagoras to
the present, will be used to help draw the boundaries
around musicology and to clarify the various schemata
within which modern musicology functions.

Finally, once the critique has been done and the
eidetic structure of musicology has been thematized, we
will project the future domain of musicology. Once the
description has produced musicology's "isness," then we
can move to what musicology should be.

NOTES FOR CHAPTER I

[1]Immanuel Kant, Kritik der reinen Vernunft, Axii.

[2]Ibid., Bxxii.

[3]Johann Nicolaus Forkel, Ueber die Theorie der Musik, insofern sie Liebhabern und Kennern nothwendig und nützlich ist (Göttingen: im Verlag der Wittwe Vandenhück, 1777).

[4]The roots of this division can be found in Aristides Quintilianus (fl AD c 200), Peri mousikes. Aristides seems to have been influenced by five sources: Damon (fl late 5th century BC), Aristoxenus (375-? BC) who was a pupil of Aristotle, Plato and the Pythagoreans. See also Marcus Meibom, Antiquae musicae auctores septem (Amstelodami: apud Ludovicum Elzevirium, 1652), p. 207.

[5]Guido Adler, "Umfang, Methode und Ziel der Musikwissenschaft," Vierteljahrsschrift für Musikwissenschaft, 1, (1885), 15-20. (Translated by David R. Lively as "Scope, Method, and Objective of Musicology.") It should be noted that the entry under "musicology" in the Harvard Dictionary of Music, ed. by Willi Apel, 2nd ed. (Cambridge, 1969), pp. 558-559 is erroneous in claiming that Adler's Musikologie (Adler: "Umfang, Methode...," p. 17) is research "and may well be considered the ingredient that turns 'musical study' into 'musicology'." (HDM, p. 558, col. 2). What Adler means by Musikologie is "comparative musicology, whose task it is to compare musical products, particularly folksongs, of various peoples, countries, and territories for ethnographic purposes, and to group and separate them according to the variety of their natures." <"...vergleichende Musikwissenschaft, die sich zur Aufgabe macht, die Tonproducte, insbesondere die Volksgesänge verschiedener Völker, Länder und Territorien behufs ethnographischer Zwecke zu vergleichen und nach der Verschiedenheit ihrer Beschaffenheit zu gruppieren und sondern." (Adler, p. 14)> In other words, ethnomusicology.

[6]Edmund Husserl, _Formal_ and _Transcendental Logic_,
trans. by Dorian Cairns (The Hague: Martinus Nijhoff,
1969), § 9, p. 36.

[7]John Stuart Mill, _A System of Logic_ (London:
Longmans, Green, 1961), § 3.

Historical study is only fruitful for the
future if it follow a powerful lifegiving
influence, for example, a new system of
culture; only, therefore, if it be guided
and dominated by a higher force, and do not
itself guide and dominate.

--Nietzsche, <u>The Use and Abuse of History</u>

CHAPTER II

A RETROSPECTIVE OF MUSICOLOGY (PART I)

§ 5.   <u>Preënlightenment</u> <u>Roots</u>

a.   <u>Some</u> <u>Ancient</u> <u>sources</u>

1.   Pythagoras, <u>fl</u>. 550 BC

In order to do an historical and descriptive study
of musicology with an eye to a critique of the discipline, we must first search the past and seek to uncover
the ideas, concepts and influences which have shaped
musicology as we know it. To begin such an inquiry I
was immediately drawn to Pythagoras, who is reputed to
have been the first music theorist, and possibly the
first musicologist, at least in the Western tradition.

Hoping not to plunge irretrievably into what W. K. C. Guthrie has called the "'bottomless pit' of research on the Pythagoreans," let us cast a glance backward at this primordial musicologist.

Pythagoras' "discovery" was twofold: we are told he found that musical intervals could be represented by numbers; and from these mathematical intervals a scale could be constructed. Pythagoras came upon this bit of mathematization from observing the ratios produced by the physical distances on the string of the monochord and the intervals produced.[1] A more romantic story has him listening to four smiths' hammers which weighed 12, 9, 8 and 6 pounds. From the beating of various combinations of the hammers, Pythagoras produced consonant intervals: the octave (12:6=2:1), the fifth (12:8=9:6=3:2), the fourth (12:9=4:3) and the whole tone (9:8).[2] The scale which Pythagoras produced is obtained from the interval of the fifth. The scale is produced as a series of five successive upper fifths and one lower fifth.[3]

This first theory of music is either the complete invention of Pythagoras or there were other influences that led him to such musical theories. There is a tradition that Pythagoras spent twelve years in Babylon where he was instructed by the magi. Iamblichus continues:

> and learned from them the most perfect
> worship of the gods. Through their assist-
> ance likewise, he arrived at the summit of
> arithmetic, music and other disciplines.[4]

Iamblichus also credits the Babylonians with the
discovery of harmonic proportion. They in turn taught
it to Pythagoras who introduced it to the Greeks.[5]
Also, Valerius Maximus and Apuleius believed that
Pythagoras learned the cosmic music in Babylon.[6] Philo
Judaeus believed that the theory of the harmony of the
spheres first arose with the Chaldaeans.[7] Farmer, in
his Historical Facts for the Arabian Musical Influence,
concludes that we should have little difficulty
accepting the evidence of Iamblicus, Philo Judaeus,
Valerius Maximus and Apuleius

> since any people who could, like the
> Babylonians, have made the very credible
> advance in arithmetical and geometrical pro-
> gressions that we know of, and who possessed
> rules for finding the areas of squares,
> rectangles, right triangles and trapezoids,
> could most certainly have devised the
> harmonical proportion and have had as com-
> plete a knowledge of the speculative theory
> of music as that possessed by the Greek theo-
> rist of music in Greece, Pythagoras.[8]

It could be argued that Mesopotamian savants formulated
a musical theory which is the starting point of our
present musical system.[9]

Another point that must be made is that these
musico-mathematical musings, whatever their source, do
not exist as pure music theory, i.e., music theory for
the sake of music alone, but belong to a much larger
cosmic concept. Pythagoras integrated his number theory

and music theory into a cosmic theory which was meant to show its structural perfection coupled with its beauty.[10] According to Censorius, Pythagoras taught that the universe was constructed according to musical ratio and that the planets emit a consonant sound as they revolve around the sun.[11]

To sum up: the Pythagorean-Mesopotamian mathematization of music in harmonics was not formulated out of a purely musical interest, but for the sake of a cosmology. Music theory was part of an explanation of the nature of the universe. The Pythagorean scale was seen as a structural element in the cosmos. This idea will be seen to be important when we consider Plato's musical ideas in the light of the artistic revolution following Athens' defeat in the Peloponnesian War. The most important concept to note is that there now exists a theoretically formulated study of music and a separate musical practice. One can theorize about the mathematical and cosmological nature of music or one can pluck away on the kithara caring little for the nature of the cosmos. The history of a dyadic relationship, which haunts us to this day, has begun.

2. Plato, 428-348 BC

Although Plato left no writings on music theory, he left several extended passages about music vis-à-vis education and society. Before we move into a discussion of Plato's ideas about music we should recall what both poetry and music meant to Plato. Grube writes:

Meantime it is essential to remember,
especially when Plato's theory of art will
seem at times to narrow down to a discussion
of poetry, that the word poietes means 'maker'
and was currently used to include every kind
of creative artist, and indeed every kind of
craftsman as well. So that even where it is
used in the more restricted sense of poet <see
Symposium 205b-c>, a wider connotation is
often vaguely present. ...The same is true
of the word mousike; at times it means music
and little else; at other times it includes
all the arts, everything connected with the
Muses...

...Plato extends the meaning of mousike,
artistic, cultured in art, far beyond itself,
to apply to the lover of all beauty, who (we
may supply the thought from later passages)
is again none other than the philosophos, the
thinker. <see Phaedo 61a>[12]

We discovered in the section on Pythagoras that a
rift developed between music theory and musical
practice. Plato addresses this bifurcation in the
Republic (530d-531c). In this passage Plato offers an
analogy that as the eyes are meant for astronomy, the
ears are meant for harmony and postulates that the two
sciences, i.e., astronomy and harmony (music) are similar as the Pythagoreans claim. The common ground
between astronomy and music is a harmony of number.
However, some people, continues Plato, reduce this science of harmony or music theory to disputes over

enharmonic tunings; whether there is a difference
between two pitches or "do the strings now render
identical sounds," i.e., unisons. This is a reduction
to musical practice. Plato adds that these practical
musicians are using their ears not their minds. There
is also a third group, which Plato does not mean to
imply in the analogy and that is those who actually
perform music, not just fight over its tunings, enharmonic or otherwise. Also, he is greatly concerned with
a developing division in musical performance itself,
i.e., between instrumental music and poetry. With the
fall of Athens in 404 there was an anti-intellectual
revolt that paralleled the rise of instrumental music.

Durant gives us an eloquent description of the
condition of Athens at the end of the Peloponnesian War.

These Greek Bourbons <Council of Thirty> had
learned nothing; they confiscated the
property and alienated the support of many
rich merchants; they plundered the temples,
sold for three talents the wharves of the
Piraeus which had cost a thousand, exiled
five thousand democrats, and put fifteen
hundred others to death; they assassinated
all Athenians who were distasteful to them
politically or personally; they put an end to
freedom of teaching, assemblage, and speech,
and Critias himself, once his pupil, forbade
Socrates to continue his public discourses.
Seeking to compromise the philosopher to
their cause, the Thirty ordered him and four
others to arrest the democrat Leon. ...

Athens was exhausted in body and soul; only
the degradation of character by prolonged war
and desperate suffering could explain the
ruthless treatment of Melos, the bitter
sentence upon Mytilene, the execution of the
Arginusae generals, and the sacrifice of
Socrates on the altar of a dying faith. All
the foundations of Athenian life were dis-
ordered: the soil of Attica had been deva-
stated by the Spartan raids, and the slow-
growing olive trees had been burned to the
ground; the Athenian navy had been destroyed,
and control of trade and the food supply had
been lost; the state treasury was empty, and
private fortunes had been taxed almost to
extinction; two thirds of the citizen body
had been killed. The damage done to Greece
by the Persian invasions could not compare
with the destruction of Greek life and property by the Peloponnesian War.[13]

That clashes of revolutions formed in such cultural and
economic chaos is understandable, and that artists,
being no less prone to change, would be caught up in the
cataclysmic dislocations in Athenian life is also
comprehensible. Under such circumstances men rail
against the Fates and the past and forge new and
different futures. Plato gives us a short history of
this musical revolution in his Laws (700a-701a). The
Athenian says:

Our music was then divided into several kinds
and patterns. One kind of song, which went

by the name of a <u>hymn</u> consisted of prayers to
the gods; there was a second and contrasting
kind which might well have been called a
<u>lament</u>; <u>paeans</u> were a third kind, and there
was fourth, the <u>dithyramb</u>, as it was called,
dealing, if I am not mistaken, with the birth
of Dionysus. ...Now these and other types
were definitely fixed, and it was not permis-
sible to misuse one kind of melody for
another. The competence to take cognizance
of these rules, to pass verdicts in accord
with them, and, in case of need, to penalize
their infraction was not left, as it is
today, to the catcalls and discordant out-
cries of the crowd, nor yet to the clapping
of applauders; the educated made it their
rule to hear the performances through in
silence... Afterward, in course of time, an
unmusical license set in with the appearance
of poets who were men of native genius, but
ignorant of what is right and legitimate in
the realm of the Muses. Possessed by a
frantic and unhallowed lust for pleasure,
they contaminated laments with hymns and
paeans with dithyrambs, actually imitated the
strains of the flute on the harp, and created
a universal confusion of forms. Thus their
folly led them unintentionally to slander
their profession by the assumption that in
music there is no such thing as a right and a
wrong, the right standard of judgment being
the pleasure given to the hearer, be he high
or low. By compositions of such a kind and

discourse to the same effect they naturally
inspired a conceit of their own competence as
judges. Thus our once silent audiences have
found a voice, in the persuasion that they
understand what is good and bad in art... If
the consequence had been even a democracy, no
great harm would have been done, so long as
the democracy was confined to art, and composed of free men. But, as things are with
us, music had given occasion to a general
conceit of universal knowledge and contempt
for law, and liberty has followed in their
.trail.

This passage, coupled with 669d-e, where a mixture of
styles is described which produces a "kind of senseless
and complicated confusion" and poets

divorce rhythm and figure from melody, by
giving metrical form to bare discourse, and
melody and rhythm from words, by their
employment of cithara and flute without vocal
accompaniment, though it is the hardest of
tasks to discover what such wordless rhythm
and tune signify, or what model worth considering they represent,

chronicles for us the degeneration of a pure classical
style into a romanticism, which mixes the modes, and the
rise of instrumental music. Along with these artistic
changes, Plato writes about the beginning of polyphony
which he finds unsuited to teaching the young: "but as
to divergence of sound and variety in the notes of the

harp, when the strings sound one tune and the composers
of the melody another, or when there results a combination of low and high notes, of slow and quick time, of
sharp and grave, and all sorts of rhythmical variations
are adopted to the notes of the lyre..." (Laws,
812d-e.). Plato offers us evidence of that ever-present
swing of artistic style from an emphasis on order, form
and harmony to what must have appeared to him as chaos.
In Nietzschean terms it is the shift from the Apollonian
to the Dionysian.

    Since Plato felt that the cosmos was constructed
according to the Forms and governed by unchanging laws,
the world and everything in it are in harmonious relationships. This doctrine was derived from the cosmological theories of the Pythagoreans who taught that the
world is of mathematical order and harmonious. When
this concept is combined with the idea that moral value
is supreme and that art should be guided by morals, a
very idealistic, moralistic and transcendent interpretation of art ensues.[14] The rôle of the poet, in this
grand cosmic harmony, is to reflect that preestablished
harmony; any deviation is a sin. The artistic changes,
no longer a reflection of cosmic order but of personal
pleasure, that took place in Plato's lifetime must have
been abhorrent to him and evidence of moral decay in
society. The Timaeus (47d-e) speaks to this harmony:

        music too, in so far as it uses audible
        sound, was bestowed for the sake of harmony,
        which has motions akin to the revolutions of
        the Soul within us, was given by the Muses to
        him who makes intelligent use of the Muses,

not as aid to irrational pleasure, as is now
supposed....

Not only was this change in musical attitudes creating
bad music, it was upsetting the harmonious nature of the
soul and the cosmos.

More specifically, Plato was thinking of the school
of Cinesias the dithyrambist which had produced
Philoxenus and Timotheus, both artistic revolution-
aries.[15] The manifesto of Timotheus of Miletus will
speak for the new artistic feeling:

I do not sing the old things,
Because the new are the winners.
Zeus the young is king today:
Once it was Cronos ruling.
Get out, old dame Music.[16]

When Plato wrote that poets attempt to make the noise of
thunder, wind, hail, cats, dogs, cattle, bird-song and
all kinds of instruments, with frequent and startling
modulations (mixing of the modes), he could have been
thinking of Timotheus' Persae which was a kind of
program music.[17]

Plato witnessed an ever-widening gulf between
theory and musical practice, between music as a reflection of cosmic harmony and music for sensuous pleasure.
This gulf widened to the point that a Greek proverb in
late antiquity "unheard music is better than heard"
shows the rift between the theorist who contemplates the
unheard and the practicing musician who plays. Theory

via harmonic science was enshrined with the truths of
astronomy. This "unheard music" was cultivated without
any regard for heard music. The idea of music became
much holier than music itself. This division is still
with us today: musicologist-theorist vis-à-vis the
performing musician. This feeling of superiority for
harmonic theory and its mathematical beauty placed
Musica as the seventh of Varro's "liberal arts"--not a
fine art, but part of the quadrivium of mathematical
subjects. "The transference of the term musica to harmonic science in itself implies that for the liberal
education music <qua practice> did not exist."[18]

3. Aristotle, 384-322 BC

Aristotle, at least in his comments about music,
takes a more mundane view of the phenomenon than his
teacher. Aristotle's concept of harmony is devoid of
any whiff of Pythagorean cosmology or Platonic eso-
tericism. His attitude toward Pythagorean number theory
is much more empirical than Plato's. The whole fabric
of Pythagorean numerology and harmonics, for Aristotle,
came from the mistaken notion that real things are
numbers.[19] Harmonics, technical music theory, is a
physical science for Aristotle and the harmoniai are
generally presented as fact and scrutinized as such.[20]
The modes, as discussed by Aristotle, were not the modes
known in the 5th century as individual and autonomous,
but as that complex of interchangeable modes and
mixtures of modes that Plato described as coming into
vogue in the 4th century.

Out of the many works in which Aristotle has
written about music or simply sound, only three, Politics, Problemata and Nicomachean Ethics, are germane to
demonstrating the divisions in music with which we are
concerned. In Politics, 1339a-1342b, Aristotle asks
whether music is merely for the sake of pleasure, or
conducive to the formation of a virtuous person, or only
for intellectual enjoyment. "It is not easy," continues
Aristotle, "to determine the nature of music, or why
anyone should have a knowledge of it."[21] This somewhat
humble statement from the omniscient Stagirite could
preface numerous tomes about music and is still a
determination not easy to make. Nevertheless, he does
agree that everyone should have some musical education,
but not to the point of making professionals out of
them. Professional musicians are vulgar and "no freeman
would play and sing unless he were intoxicated or in
jest."[22] Again he speaks indirectly to the division
between professional musicians and dilettantes:

> The right measure <of musical education> will
> be attained if students of music stop short
> of the arts which are practiced in profes-
> sional contests, and do not seek to acquire
> those fantastic marvels of execution which
> are now the fashion in such contests, and
> from these have passed into education.[23]

Not only should one not become such a professional, but
Aristotle leaves us with the impression that "those
fantastic marvels of execution," probably highly technical passage work and modulation techniques, are new phenomena for mixing modes and that people were being

taught them as a matter of course. He goes on to reject
such teaching and using professional instruments such as
the flute and harp, the main reason being that profes-
sionalism's purpose is to give pleasure of a vulgar sort
and not personal improvement.[24] How does music improve
us? By giving us intellectual enjoyment and leisure,
not vulgar pleasure.[25] At 1339b Aristotle gives a
passing nod to the existence of instrumental music:
"All men agree that music is one of the pleasantest
things whether with or without song...." No condemna-
tion, no fear of a tear in the cosmic fabric, just the
fact that it exists and that it is pleasant. Earlier in
the same section, Aristotle suggests that there was a
division between those who "practice" and those who
"hear others." This would seem to mean that there were
those who had no practical musical education at all,
which would be at variance with classical tradition.
One could interpret this passage to mean that there were
those who played music and those who wrote music theory
(harmonics). It is possible that the Greek music theory
bequeathed to us could be at odds with Greek musical
practice. This should not seem too strange; even today,
composers do not write the way theory books report music
to be.

The Problemata[26], the second work to be considered,
are constructed as a series of questions about certain
problems. They range from such things as Sweat and
Unpleasant Smells (Bks. II & XIII) to Mathematical
Theory and Harmony (Bks. XV & XIX). Most of the questions in each set of problems have direct answers, but
some are answered with another question. In the set of
problems on harmony, the questions extend from the

mundane: "Why do those who are sad and those who are enjoying themselves both have the flute played to them? <Ans.> Is it because the latter class hope to lessen their grief, and the former to increase their pleasure?"; to the theoretical: "Why is nete double hypate? <Ans.> First of all is it because the string when struck at half its length gives an octave with the string struck at full length?"[27]

There are two paragraphs of the Problemata that give evidence to the furcations that occurred in Greek music in the 4th century. In para. 15, <Aristotle> contrasts an older singing style with a newer, professional style. He compares an antistrophic composition, which he calls simple, with the nomes which are delivered by professional musicians. The whole passage is a comparison of the music of the "old days" and the newer music which constituted a change in style and performance practice. One of the major changes is that the dithyrambs became imitative and written with variations. <Aristotle> could mean by this that the imitation is on the level that Plato mentioned in the Republic (397a-b) where composers are said to try and imitate all types of animal sounds. The variations alluded to in the <Aristotelian> text were probably melismatic in nature. Instrumental music is only hinted at in para. 27 as a point of fact, but is used in another context:

Why is what is heard the only object of perception which has moral character? For every tune, even if it has no words, has

nevertheless character; but neither colour,
smell nor flavour have it.

The third and last section to be taken up comes from two
different parts of the Nicomachean Ethics (1170a and
1105a, trans. W. D. Ross). Aristotle writes:

> With others therefore his <the happy man's>
> activity will be more continuous, and it is
> in itself pleasant, as it ought to be for the
> man who is supremely happy; for a good man
> qua good delights in virtuous actions and is
> vexed at vicious ones, as a musical man
> enjoys beautiful tunes but is pained at bad
> ones.

And further:

> The question might be asked, what we mean by
> saying that we must become just by doing just
> acts, and temperate by doing temperate acts;
> for if men do just and temperate acts, they
> are already just and temperate, exactly as,
> if they do what is in accordance with the
> laws of grammar and of music, they are
> grammarians and musicians.

How do these two extracts speak to our projects? In the
first quotation, Aristotle inquires about the relationship between pleasure and goodness. The answer involves
a musical analogy. The happy man enjoys virtuous acts
and hates evil ones just as the musical man "enjoys
beautiful tunes but is pained at bad ones." So in the

second passage: just and temperate acts are done by
just and temperate men, as a man who writes music in
accordance with musical law is a musician. The
adjectives "good" and "bad" and the implications of
"just" are not ethical but technical terms. They
betoken the person trained in music either as
theoretician or professional performer. Again, we
have evidence of the emergence of a class of professionals distinct from a class of dilettantes.

In sum: Plato can be seen as a reactionary
artistically. His attempts to standardize and legalize
poetic production in the Republic; his almost wistful
musings about the artistic past and a desire to bring
it back in the Laws; his derisive writings about the
new music in the Gorgias; and his adherence to a
Pythagorean cosmology all point to a reversionary
attitude. Aristotle, on the other hand, is revolu-
tionary not reactionary. He is in the artistic avant-
garde. He, generally, describes and does not prescribe
artistic conventions. He attempts a transvaluation of
music-poetry by decosmologizing them and placing them
on an empirical footing, not the quasi-mystical one found
in Plato.

All of the divisions and subdivisions that occurred
in music from Pythagoras to the time of Aristoxenus
(c.375-?) are schematized in the following figure:

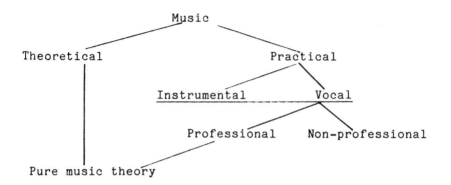

Fig. 1. Divisions in music from Pythagoras
         to Aristotle

4. Aristoxenus, 375-? BC

Aristoxenus, according to the Suidas, a 10th-
century lexicon, wrote 453 books, of which only four on
music have come down to us, and those in fragments.
They are: 1) Harmonics (three parts); 2) Introduction
to Harmonics (a fragment); 3) Banqueting Miscellanies
(found only in Plutarch); and, 4) Elements of
Eurhythmics (known from a later transcription).
Aristoxenus' father was a professional musician from the
town of Tarentum in Italy, which was known for keeping
alive the old artistic ways; he trained his son in the
classical art. The musical knowledge gained in this
training, coupled with his study of logic with
Aristotle, led him to write a scientific description of
Greek music theory up through the 4th century. The
major difference between Aristoxenus' theory and all
other musical theorists is that they were mathematical,
i.e., started from a series of notes as fixed points on

an hypothetical gamut, and his was grounded in logical
induction based on observation of the human voice in
action.

Aristoxenus was a musical reactionary who disliked
the new polyphony and variation techniques being used
and who was opposed to musical innovation. There were
two contrary musical views current in his time: the
older school, stemming from the Pythagoreans, which saw
a mathematical-cosmological significance in music and
Platonic ethical theory; and, second, that music merely
tickles the ear--the Sophists generally held to this
view. Aristoxenus did believe in the ethical nature of
music, but felt it was to be discovered not in mysticism
or mathematics. Instead it was to be found in the
tickling process, i.e., via a positivistic, psychological, physiological approach. Out of this approach comes
an important concept, to rear its head again in Kant and
the phenomenologists: the locus of meaning is not to be
found in the things judged but in the act of judgment.

Of the four extant books on music, by far the most
important is the Harmonics.[28] Instead of taking the
reader through the work section by section, thereby
confusing the issue, I have categorized the pertinent
texts and will discuss them according to these categories: method, instrumental vis-à-vis vocal music;[29]
old style contrasted to new style; older musical
writings and where they went astray; and differences
between theory and practice.

Aristoxenus opens the Harmonics by letting us know
that part of his method is to "divide and conquer." The

science of melody is divided into several special
sciences; the one we are going to pursue is called
"harmonic," which he defines as "all that relates to the
theory of scales and keys." <1> He approaches the study
of scales and modes as a scientific investigation of the
human voice. <3> In other words, as Aristotle would no
doubt recommend, we start with phenomena and we observe.
As Aristoxenus states at 33, we "appeal to the two
faculties of hearing and intellect." Later on he outlines his method in full:

> Firstly, the phenomena themselves must be
> correctly observed; secondly, what is prior
> and what is derivative in them must be
> properly discriminated; thirdly, our conclu-
> sions and inferences must follow legitimately
> from the premises. And as in every science
> that consists of several propositions the
> proper course is to find certain principles
> from which to deduce the dependent truth, we
> must be guided in our selection of principles
> by two considerations. Firstly, every
> proposition that is to serve as a principle
> must be true and evident; secondly, it must
> be such as to be accepted by the sense-
> perception as one of the primary truths of
> Harmonic science. <43-44>

This method is a far cry from the mystico-mathematical
interpretations of earlier philosophers--Aristoxenus
does not miss this point! If the method described above
is any indication of methods commonly used, their dis-
appearance in Plotinian emanations can only be lamented.

In his method, Aristoxenus calls on accurate
observation of phenomena; this of course is the ground
of any scientific method. Second, he calls for a
determination of cause and effect. Since he is dealing
with scales and modes, he might use something like Mill's
method of agreement to determine the fundamental scalar
patterns and then be able to delineate the derivatives
of those scales. Such a method must have been used by
Aristotle in his description of tragedy in the Poetics.
Third, Aristoxenus wants our findings to be formulated
according to the rules of logic. The propositions in
our logical formulation must meet two criteria: they
must be true and evident; and, they must be grounded in
experience, i.e., sense-perception.

The two places in the Harmonics where instrumental
music is mentioned are just that: an imitation and a
mention. Instrumental music exists, thus it must be
mentioned. The first statement is in the introductory
section where Aristoxenus states that any "profound
speculation" on scales and modes must take into account
when they "are enlisted in the service of poetry." <1>
This sounds as if there were in his day more instrumental music than vocal, or at least his contemporaries
were ignoring vocal music (poetry) in their writings.
He goes on to say that "our subject matter then being
all melody, whether vocal or instrumental, our method
rests in the last resort on an appeal to the two
faculties of hearing and intellect." <33>

Our third category, the old vs. the new music,
reminds one of Plato's Laws[30] where he describes a style
coming into vogue which mixed modes and which produced a

"kind of senseless and complicated confusion."
Aristoxenus speaks to this stylistic change in several
passages. In discussing the characteristics of melody
he writes: "every melody must be Diatonic, or
Chromatic, or Enharmonic, or blended of these kinds, or
composed of what they have in common." <44> This is a
clear statement on the existence of the mixed-modes of
the new music mentioned by Plato. Modulation from one
mode or mixed-mode to another was common, but was
uncommon in Hellenic music. Aristoxenus tells us that
his work is the first to take up the question of modulation <38>, possibly because, heretofore, the question
had not been raised. The new style also presented the
theorist with variation, probably melismatic in nature.
Aristoxenus considered variations "new ground, as there
is in existence no previous treatment of them worth
mentioning." <4> The longest excerpt concerning the
juxtaposition of styles is at 23. In this selection he
shows himself to be a musical reactionary. He even
complains that his contemporaries do not know ancient
music. To quote him in full:

> That there is a style of composition which
> demands a Lichanus at a distance of two tones
> from the Mese, and that far from being
> contemptible it is perhaps the noblest of
> styles--this is a truth which is indeed far
> from patent to most musical students of
> today, though it would become so if they were
> led to the apprehension of it by the aid of
> concrete examples. But to anyone who
> possesses an adequate acquaintance with the
> first and second styles of ancient music, it

is indisputable truth. Theorists who are
only familiar with the style of composition
now in vogue naturally exclude the two-tone
Lichanus, the prevailing tendency being to
the use of the higher Lichani. <23>

Aristoxenus' predecessors do not get off lightly
either. According to him, all previous studies of music
have fallen short, presumably because they were not
scientific, and nowhere as complete as his. <36-37>
Specifically, even though Aristoxenus does not mention
them by name, it is not difficult to read his mind:
Pythagoras and Plato are soundly refuted, fundamentally
for their use of number theory and mysticism and not
"science" as a ground for musical study. Aristoxenus
insisted that the study of music must be empirical,
grounded in the phenomena, for answers to be true. He
clearly writes:

And for our answers we endeavor to supply
proofs that will be in agreement with the
phenomena--in this unlike our predecessors.
For some of these introduced extraneous
reasonings, and rejecting the senses as
inaccurate fabricated rational principles,
asserting that height and depth of pitch
consist in certain numerical ratios and
relative rates of vibration--a theory
utterly extraneous to the subject and quite
at variance with the phenomena; while others,
dispensing with reason and demonstration,
confined themselves to isolated dogmatic

statements, not being successful either in
their enumeration of the mere phenomena. <32>

It is obvious from this extract that, at least in one
place, Aristoxenus was led astray by his method and pure
number speculation was proven right: height and depth of
pitch do consist in certain numerical ratios and rates
of vibration. Perhaps he can be forgiven this observational and methodological lapse, not having the instruments with which to measure pitch. Nevertheless,
another clear and distinct appeal to observation as
against cosmological speculation is made at 42-43:

> To suppose, because one sees day by day the
> finger-holes the same and the strings at the
> same tension, that one will find in these har-
> mony with it, permanence and eternally immuta-
> ble order--this is sheer folly. For us there
> is no harmony in the strings save that which
> the cunning of the hand confers upon them....

In this point, undoubtedly, Aristoxenus is right. No
universal law dictates the tuning of any instrument, nor
can such a law be read when one finds a tuned instrument.

The last category, and one of the more important
ones for our project, is the rising distinction between
music theory and musical practice. Aristoxenus informs
us that there are all kinds of mistakes being made about
"harmonics," both from the theoretical side and from the
practical. He even hints that the two sometimes do not
meet.

> Some consider Harmonic, a sublime science,
> and expect a course of it to make them
> musicians; nay some even conceive it will
> exalt their moral nature. ... Some regard
> Harmonic as quite a thing of no importance,
> and actually prefer to remain totally unac-
> quainted even with its nature and aim. <31>

Just studying music theory will not make a musician out
of you, and by the same token you cannot just play and
ignore theory and also expect to be a musician. Knowledge about scales and modes (harmonics) is only a part
of the knowledge any musician should have. He should
also know the rhythmic modes, meter and instrumentation.
Even so, one could be a savant in all three areas and
still not be a practicing musician. <32> Aristoxenus is
describing the pure music theorist, the one not concerned with applied music. This is a distinction still
made in our universities: you study music theory or
applied music, e.g., piano, flute, etc.; you rarely do
both. In a somewhat obscure passage, Aristoxenus
differentiates between an abstract theoretical point of
view and a practical standpoint. When discussing the
fractions of a tone, he tells us that there are three:
halftone (semi-tone); third-tone (smallest chromatic
diesis); and quarter-tone (smallest enharmonic diesis).
He says that a misunderstanding exists concerning these
divisions, which "is due to their <musicians'> not
observing that to employ the third part of a tone is a
very different thing from dividing a tone into three
parts and singing all three. Second, from an abstract
<theoretical> point of view, no doubt, we regard no
interval as the smallest possible." <46> The human ear

can distinguish a finite number of microtones, but
theoretically the half-tone is infinitely divisible.

The Harmonics contains much more than we have
discussed. It constitutes nearly the sum of all that is
known about ancient Greek music and is only about scales
and modes. The work is a highly technical description
of these scales and modes in use in the early
Hellenistic era. From the extant musical writings of
Aristoxenus, Paul Marquard has schematized the parts and
divisions of musical knowledge.[31] (See Fig. 2 on next
page; the similarities with Fig. 1 above are obvious.)

From this moment on music studies tend to be a
remastication of the musical knowledge of the quartet we
have studied, theoreticians taking one of two roads
offered by them: the mystical or the empirical. The
overriding influence exercised by these writers was due
less to an understanding of their work than to the
extreme authority of their names. Practical music lost
any intellectual influence it might have had in Hellenic
times. Yet the two sciences of philosophy and harmonics
reigned on. In due time harmonics usurped the title
"music" and any late Greek theorist will use the term
"music" in this more restricted sense.

KNOWLEDGE OF MUSIC

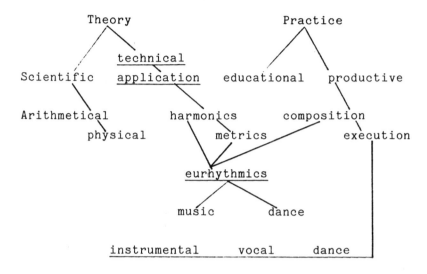

Fig. 2. Aristoxenus schematized by Marquard

Before moving on to the last two ancient authors
to be considered, Ptolemy and Aristides Quintilianus, it
might be wise to cast a glance forward. I do this
because the foundation for the discipline we know as
musicology has solidified and will change little in the
telling. As our project progresses, we will find that
the modern bifurcation of musicology into historical and
systematic is traceable to these Greeks. The theoretical side of music which, as we saw, quickly divorced
itself from musical practice is what is known as systematic musicology, i.e., music theory. What we call
historical musicology, or, in the minds of some, simply
musicology, arose when writers became interested, historically speaking, in the practical side of our music
dyad and then began to report on musical practices.

The 400 or more years that elapsed between
Aristoxenus and Klaudios Ptolemaios (AD 83-161) saw
little original music theory being written.
Eratosthenes (284-202 BC), who is best known as a
geographer, wrote a mathematical theory of music called
the Platonikos which attempts to synthesize music theory
and the cosmic theories in Plato's Timaeus.   Arius
Didymus (fl. AD 40-60) was the primary authority for
Ptolemy and Ptolemy's commentator Porphyry.   Arius
Didymus' works exist only in fragments.   These fragments
lead us to believe that his work relies heavily on
Aristoxenus, especially regarding method: the use of
reason coupled with sense perception.   This whole period
was a flux of two major interpretations of music: the
Pythagorean vs. the Aristoxenian, i.e., mysticism vs.
empiricism.

5.   Ptolemy, 83-161

Ptolemy can count among his astronomical
contributions a three-volume work called the
Harmonikon.[32]   From a methodological standpoint Ptolemy
"corrected" Aristoxenus by reintroducing mathematics, in
a demythologized form, into the mainstream of music
theory.   Ptolemy had two criteria for judgment: reason
and empirical observation; these two were not to contra-
dict each other.   Knowing that sense perception, the
source of his empirical observations, is fallible, he
desired a scientific instrument with which to measure
the numerical ratios of musical intervals; this instrument was the monochord.   One came to the concepts of
music theory via precise mathematical calculations using

instruments such as the monochord. Also, Ptolemy used
the authority of Arius Didymus to show the differences
between the Pythagoreans and the Aristoxenians (bk. I,
§ 5-11): Pythagoreans, whose musical theories do not
correspond to musical reality, and the mistake of
Aristoxenus is in not using precise mathematics to
demonstrate interval ratios. It is ironical that
Ptolemy was to turn around and make the same judgment as
the Pythagoreans: constructing musical systems with
little basis in reality. The bulk of Ptolemy's work is
purely technical except for § 3-16 of Book III where he
attempts to explain the relationship of musical notes to
the human soul; and, unable to keep Pythagoras at bay,
he explains the relationship between notes and heavenly
bodies by drawing on his astronomy <§ 8-16>.

   At this point music theory and musical practice
are widely divergent. Ptolemy and a whole host of
"harmonists" used mathematics for interval measurement
for no practical purpose at all. Even thought some of
them might match current usage, Ptolemy lists scale
after scale which never existed in the real musical
world. These tonoi, found in Ptolemy, do not agree with
the name given to kitharists' tunings in his day.
Theorists used an academic fifteen-stringed kithara
which was constructed to suit their own hypothetical
gamut with little thought to musical practice. Whatever
these academic tonoi meant, their Ptolemaic names and
notations show how far musical practice had moved away
from theory. As Johannes Lohmann writes: "Its
nomenclature <musical notations> is that of geometry,
thus it is borrowed from a rigorously scientific
designation and has nothing to do with practice."[33]

6. Aristides Quintilianus, <u>fl</u>. AD 200

<u>Peri</u> <u>mousike</u> of Aristides Quintilianus relies
heavily on Ptolemy and Aristoxenus for its ideas and
content. The work is in three books: 1) is concerned
with harmonic, rhythmic and metrical theory which is
borrowed from Aristoxenus and unknown Alexandrian metri-
cians; 2) is on the ethical and paideutic aspects of
music which he refers, with deference, to Plato and to
the doctrines of the Periclean Damon; and, 3) sets out
the numerical and cosmological relationships in which he
thought music was involved, all cast in neo-Pythagorean
and neo-Platonic terms.

For our purposes, Aristides Quintilianus gives the
first schema of musical knowledge (see Fig. 3, below).
This schema clearly shows the division between the theoretical and practical aspects of music. The importance
of this classification system cannot be overemphasized
because it forms the nucleus of Guido Adler's
<u>Musikwissenschaft</u> schema of 1885.[34] A glance at Figs.
1-3 will show the genesis of a divided musicology.

Before moving to a conclusion of these ancient
sources it remains to mention two contemporaries of
Aristides Quintilianus: Cleonides and Athenaeus.
Cleonides wrote a book called the <u>Eisagoge</u> <u>harmonike</u>[35]
in which he simplified and summarized the theories of
Aristoxenus. This work is important because it is
through a Latin translation (1497) by Georgius Valla
that the Renaissance gleaned most of its information
about ancient Greek music.

I.   Theoretikon (theoretical or speculative part)
      A. physikon (physical-scientific)
          a. arithmetike (arithmetic)
          b. physike (physics)
      B. technikon (special-technical)
          a. harmonike (harmony)
          b. rhythmike (rhythm)
          c. metrike (versification)
II.   praktikon paideutikon (instruction or practice)
      A. chrestikon (theory of composition)
          a. melopoiia (melic composition)
          b. rhythmopoiia (applied rhythmics)
          c. poiesis (poetics)
      B. exaggeltikon (practice; lit. "discovered")
          a. organike (instrumental playing)
          b. oidike (song)
          c. hypokritike (dramatic action)

Fig. 3. Aristides Quintilianus' System of Music

Athenaeus contributed the Deipnosophistai,[36]
Sophists at Dinner. This work, of which we possess
fifteen of thirty books, is not technical, but is an
example of "historical musicology" in chatty format.
Athenaeus reports a variety of stories about music and
how famous men used music to calm anger and other
emotions, much as the Homeric Achilles calmed himself
with the kithara. He also relates the ethical-moral
character of the harmonies, much as Plato did, with the
sociological twist of musing that if the Ionian harmony
is austere and hard, it is because the Ionians, who
originated the harmony, are austere and hard. Athenaeus

talks much about the music of "olden times" when music
was brave and noble, unlike today

> when practically all the ancient customs fell
> into decay, this devotion to principle
> ceased, and debased fashions in music came to
> light, wherein everyone who practised them
> substituted effeminacy for gentleness, and
> license and looseness for moderation.[37]

In concluding this section let us review some of
the evidence used to support the ancient split in music
that is the basis of contemporary musicology. First, a
great deal of confusion, both ancient and modern, exists
on the function and meaning of the tonoi. As this word
first appears in 4th-century harmonic theory it was used
as a verb to describe the stringing and tuning of
instruments. As a noun, tonoi, it is never used by
composers and never means melodic style or melodic
patterns. When used in a compound it means the tension
of the voice, not pitch. However, contrary to practice,
theorists used the word to mean the continuous double-
octave scale in all the genera. The only possible
reason for this difference in usage is the unbounded
ability of the early Hellenistic writers to produce
abstract entities with no factual basis from mere words.
Second, by the Alexandrian period these tonoi had meta-
morphosed into sets of fifteen tonoi for each semitone.
They came in sets with hypothetical names, such as
Hypodorian--Dorian--Hyperdorian, which were completely
anomalous as most of them do not agree with the name
given to kitharists' tunings at this time. Third, Greek
notation-systems must have been a theoretical device to

convey the hypothetical _tonoi_. This notation, from
what is known about it, would probably be unusable to
the practical musician because it does not define the
function of the notes nor the size of the intervals.
Lastly, the divisions found in Aristoxenus show clearly
the early division of music along theoretical and
practical lines.

Some closing thoughts and speculations: there
seems to be a propensity in Greek thought about music,
if not things in general, to start from what can only be
called an a _priori_ or metaphysical foundation. With
Pythagoras it was the function of mathematics which
revealed to him the secrets of the intervals and of the
cosmos. Because of the universal nature of numbers,
music quickly became a vital part in a cosmology ruled
by number. For Plato, music, in its Pythagorean guise,
became the voice of the order in the universe, an order
not to be disturbed by professional innovation. With a
stretch of the speculative imagination, Plato could be
seen as the first historical musicologist. In the
Republic he reports on the changes in musical style and,
more specifically, in the _Laws_ he engages in normative
musicology, i.e., he sets up the rules and regulations
by which music is to be written. He is rarely systematic (theoretical) in the way <Aristotle> or Aristoxenus
are. Aristotle brought to musical studies an empirical
bent. Even here, as we see in his pupil Aristoxenus
(Aristotle once accused him of excessive clarity), this
empiricism replaced the earlier mystico-mathematical a
priori with that of logical induction which has its own
mystique. Aristoxenus thought that music must be
studied without the aid of mathematics which had been

tainted with Pythagoreanism. Ptolemy, as we saw,
attempted to demythologize mathematics and bring it back
into the fold as a means of measurement via the monochord. But the a priori, like some chimera in the dark
corners of the human mind, reasserts itself as an hypothetical (mathematical) scale. This scale, used as a
measuring tool, passed judgment on musical realities.
This process, building a theory, then trying to force
reality to conform, has been repeated countless times
throughout the history of musical studies. Even today
students are taught the "perfect" sonata-allegro form
not knowing such a creature is the fabrication of musical theorists from innumerable examples of sonata form
movements and that no such ideal form exists. The same
can be said of school-book fugues. Nowhere in fugal
literature do you find such beasts. Such concepts
(which may have pedagogical importance) become hin-
drances to comprehension when they have been erected
into sacred cows, and musical practice is judged "good" or
"bad" to the degree real music conforms to the text books.
What the Greeks started, we continue.

Let me end, finally, our antique ruminations on a
somewhat pessimistic but Platonic note. In the
Philebus, Plato has Socrates make the following comment
about music:

> Take music first; it is full of this; it
> attains harmony by guesswork, based on
> practice, not by measurement; and flute music
> throughout tries to find the pitch of each
> note as it is produced by guess, so that

> the amount of uncertainty mixed up in it is
> great, and the amount of certainty is
> small.[38]

We could say the same about our knowledge of Greek
music theory.

b. Early Middle Ages

Medieval musical knowledge was grounded in the
music theory of the ancients as transmitted by St.
Augustine (354-430) and Boëthius (c. 480-525). Both
these writers were familiar with ancient Greek music
theory through the work of writers like Ptolemy and
Aristides Quintilianus. Nearly every medieval musical
theorist that came after Augustine and Boëthius either
paraphrased or copied them word for word, e.g., Regino
of Prüm (d. 915), in his De Harmonica Institutione,
copied whole sections of Boëthius. Each succeeding
century produced many such music treatises. These
medieval musical works can be divided, in ancient
fashion, into two broad categories: practical and theoretical. For the first time we have works appearing
that are meant solely for the training of music students
and professional musicians, e.g., the Musica Disciplina
of Aurelian of Réomé (fl. c. 850). Theoretical works
abound. There are those that are completely devoted to
music such as the De Institutione Musica of Boëthius;
and there are those general, some encyclopedic, works
which contain sections on music, e.g., the De Musica of
Cassiodorus (c. 490-c. 575) and the Etymologiae of
Isidore of Seville (c. 570-636).

Not only were there music theory books and
encyclopedia entries under music, many medieval philosophers wrote about music. Since music was considered one
of the mathematical sciences, along with astronomy,
arithmetic and geometry, philosophy being their mother,
medieval philosophers judged music an integral part of
their philosophies.[39] Such men as Robert Grosseteste
and Roger Bacon, Thomas Aquinas and Bonaventura all
treated of music in their writings.

The fundamental idea, drawn from the ancients, _pace_
Aristoxenus, is that music is essentially proportion and
number. For example, a ground rule of Cassiodorus was,
musica est _disciplina_, _quae_ de _numeris_ loquitur, which
was followed by all subsequent writers who looked upon
music as more closely akin to mathematical science than
to art.

Music, to these medieval writers, still had that
broad, ancient meaning: wherever there is harmony there
is music, and harmony does not always express itself
aurally. As a matter of fact, most medieval theorists
were not interested in sound, but in abstract harmony
and proportion. This preoccupation was to culminate in
some fantastic temporal proportions that could never be
reproduced in the real musical world. This abstract
musical concept, as we have seen, comes directly from
the Pythagoreans, from Plato's _Timaeus_ (this was the
only Platonic dialogue available, in Latin, to these
writers), and, as we shall see, from Boëthius.

Proportion being central to music, as the author of
Musica _Enchiriadis_ writes:

> All that is sweetness in melody is produced
> by number by means of fixed relationships;
> all that is pleasant in rhythms, either in
> melodies or in rhythmical movements, derives
> exclusively from number; sounds pass quickly,
> but numbers remain;[40]

and number and proportion not being of human production,
as Regino of Prüm says, "one should realize that the
harmonies discussed here were not invented by the human
mind, but revealed to Pythagoras by divine consent;"[41]
the theory of music was seen as being a part of
ontology:

> the same principle which regulates the
> concord of voices also governs the nature of
> mortals. The same numerical relationships
> which determine the concord of unequal sounds
> also determine the concord of life and body,
> the concord of adverse elements and the
> central harmony of the whole universe.[42]

Since music qua ontology is part of the very fiber of
the being of the cosmos, its apprehension is not only
aural but also mental or psychical. John Scotus
Eriugena, in his De Divisione Naturae, speaks to this
very quality of the mathematical universality of music:

> I am convinced that nothing pleases the soul
> and nothing produces beauty but the rational
> intervals of different sounds, which, grouped
> together, produce the sweetness of musical
> melody. It is not the various sounds which

produce the sweetness of the harmony, but the
relationships of the sounds and their proportions, which are perceived and judged by
the inner sense of the soul.[43]

This wide concept of music was divided into three parts:
musica insrumentalis, musica humana and musica mundana
(these will be treated in more detail when considering
Boëthius). Again, these divisions are neo-Pythagorean
and many writers of the Middle Ages attributed them to
Pythagoras himself.

Concomitant with this threefold musical division,
as musicians theorize, compose and perform, there were
two kinds of musicians: the practical and the theoretical. These two correspond to the two basic attitudes we
have been tracing as the ground of modern musicology:
musica practica and musica theoretica, speculativa.
Dominicus Gundissalinus (fl. 1150) describes the
distinction thus:

> an artist in the practical sense is the man
> who arranges neumata and harmonies, and his
> active task is to compose...an artist in the
> theoretical sense is the man who teaches us
> how this is to be done in accordance with
> art.[44]

The theoretical musician only acquired knowledge about
music, but music in the wide sense, thus it was included
in the study of geometry and logic.

Most often this term "musician" (musicus) belonged
just to the theoretician not the practicing musician,
who was more often than not called cantor. Regino of
Prüm describes the distinction: "the name of musician
is not given to the man who merely practices music with
his hands."[45] John Cotton, in his Musica, speaks to
this difference with an amusing analogy:

> The musician and the singer differ
> considerably from one another: for while
> the musician, by virtue of his art, always
> acts appropriately, the singer owes the
> appropriate way which he sometimes goes
> exclusively to practice. To whom can I
> better compare the singer than to the
> drunkard who, while returning home, is
> completely ignorant of which way he is
> going.[46]

Letting the foregoing remarks suffice as a
prolegomenon to music studies in the Middle Ages, let us
move to consider in closer detail a few of the more
prominent writers on music from the period.

1. St. Augustine, 354-430

St. Augustine lived at a time when the old order
was dying and a new age was being born. It was from his
hand that much ancient musical and aesthetic thought was
given to this new age. He was thoroughly educated in
the Hellenistic-Roman fashion and inherited the knowledge of Hellenistic thinkers. His aesthetics was a

mixture of Stoicism, Cicero, Plato, Plotinus and others.
Out of this eclectic aesthetics the most important concept to be passed on, especially for our project, is
that of beauty qua proportion and measure. From
the Pythagoreans he took mathematics in all of its
trappings, from Platonic tradition absolute beauty.

The work where this concept of measure is most
obvious is in his dialogue De Musica.[47] The De Musica
as it has come to us is a fragment. It was a fragment
to Augustine also, as he never finished the work. Out
of a six-book opus we have five on rhythm and one, the
last book, which is of more interest to us, concerning
the hierarchy of number and a cosmology. Since we
possess only fragments of Aristoxenus' work on harmony
and no treatise on rhythm from any ancient hand, these
books of Augustine are our earliest source on ancient
rhythmical and metrical ideas. It is believed he wanted
to write six more books on melody which would have been
a classical treatise on harmonics.

Augustine tells us that there are five kinds of
rhythm. He is concerned with a rhythmic concept far
broader than our ideas about rhythm. He writes in book
VI:

> Of the five kinds of rhythm, let the first be
> called rhythm of judgment, the second rhythm
> of action, the third rhythm of perception,
> the fourth rhythm of memory, and the fifth
> rhythm of sounds.[48]

Earlier in the book, chapter 2, Augustine clarifies this
somewhat enigmatic statement. The fifth kind of rhythm
(sounds) consists in audial impressions which please if
they are regular, and displease if irregular. Memory is
mere remembrance of things heard. One hears sounds
which the soul experiences in the body when it is under
the influence of sound. Judgment is passed on all of
these "on the strength of some natural laws accepting it
or rejecting it."[49] As we have seen, harmony is anything that fits well together, so it seems that anything
that moves well has rhythm.

Book VI concerns music in its cosmological and
theological aspects and clearly stems from the last book
of Aristides Quintilianus and from the tradition of
Plato's Timaeus. Augustine does not speak at all to
contemporary musical practice in this book. His concern
is with the beauty of number removed from anything so
transient as spoken poetry or heard music. Augustine
continues by posing the question: when we write poetry
(which would include the music) do we use number in
devising the verse? The student responds:

> I cannot imagine it otherwise.
> And do you think that these numbers, what ever
> they are, pass away together with the poetry,
> or remain?
> They certainly remain.
> So you must agree that transient numbers are
> made from certain lasting numbers.[50]

The whole tone of this book is summed up in its
superscription: "the mind is raised from the

consideration of changeable numbers in inferior things
to unchangeable numbers in unchangeable truth itself."[51]

Finally, Augustine defines music in Book I, and it
is a definition that will follow music around throughout
this whole period and into the Renaissance: "Music is
the science of mensurating well."[52] This definition is
much more concerned with the measured or mathematical
aspects of music than the practical. Nowhere in the De
Musica does Augustine write about the practice of music
in his day.

2.   Martianus Capella, fl. c. 420

Martianus Capella wrote an allegory De Nuptiis
Philologiae et Mercurii, libri IX,[53] the last book of
which is on harmony <§ 888-1000>. The work was lost
almost as soon as it was written, only to be discovered
in the 9th century and commented on by John Scotus
Eriugena, Marin of Laon and Rémy of Auxerre. In this
form the work received wide circulation and authority in
the Carolingian Renaissance.

The work is cast in the form of an allegory in
which philology and Mercury are wedded in the presence
of the gods and sundry others. Speeches are made about
the liberal arts and at the end of the work Harmonia
speaks her piece. This speech is a flourish of baroque-
like prose in which nothing is said about contemporary
musical practice, unless it be celestial musical practice. One example will suffice; there are pages of such
prose: "Thus Venus spoke and, lying backward,

leaned into the embrace of Pleasure, who was standing by her....Then, as she reclined gracefully, and her relaxed attitude added to her charm, Mars gave her a tender and admiring glance from afar, and in a faltering and feeble voice he too commended her, and then was seen to draw a deep breath" <§ 889>. Embedded in this flurry of godly chatter, Martianus waxes informative <§ 936-995>. Yet, this part is not original, for it is a translation, with changes, omissions and insertions of parts of the work on music by Aristides Quintilianus.

Harmonia instructs the assembled celestials in the basic terminology of music, its classification, rhythm and meter and, last of all, the ethical effects of music. All of this is prefaced with a convoluted history of the rôle of music in the godly realm and why mankind was ever given knowledge about harmony <§ 888-920>. Music has a simple classification scheme: "it is harmony or rhythm or meter" <§ 936>. At § 968 rhythm is described as an abstract concept; it is the form of motion, and only becomes rhythmic in practice. Harmonia repeats a classification system and set of definitions said to stem from Lasus of Hermione (6th century BC) in which music is divided into subject matter (melody, measures, words), practice (composition) and exposition (interpretation) <§ 936-962>. This is the same style division we have seen all along--subject matter being theoretical and practice-exposition being practical.

3. Boëthius, 480-524

The De Institutione Musica of Anicius Manlius
Torquatus Severinus Boëthius is a free translation,
compilation and paraphrase of numerous texts.[54] In
spite of the fact that Cassiodorus tells us that
Boëthius' work is a translation of Pythagoras, it is
not.[55] Boëthius, in fact, did not draw from any single
work, except his own De Institutione Arithmetica, which
was used for the purely mathematical parts of the musical treatise, e.g., the greater part of Book II. There
are, however, many ancient authors to whom Boëthius
gives credit: Plato, Cicero, Statius, Aristotle,
Ptolemy, Pythagoras, Nicomachus, Aristoxenus, to name a
few.[56] This list of authors should suffice to show his
debt and reliance on and transmission of ancient Greek
music theory.

The Boëthian text covers a wide range of musical
subjects and many that we could claim as being outside
the purview of music. Book I contains the elements of
music, its classification, general introduction to proportion and its relationship to the Pythagoreans.
Physiology and sound propagation are discussed in
chapter XIX: "How One Hears" where Boëthius proposes
that sound is frequencies, waves in the air, that beat
against the ear drum. Book I continues with a technical
discussion of music theory and ends with a definition of
"what a musician is." This definition will be discussed
in a moment.

Book II is a more fully explained version of Book
I, which is merely an exposition of musical topics. To

this explanation Boëthius adds a chapter on Pythagorean philosophy and a great deal of mathematics taken from his work on arithmetic. The remaining three books continue this explanation of musical science with presentations and refutations of some of the ideas of Aristoxenus and Ptolemy.

More than any previous writer he gives precedence to the music theoretician over the performer. As the following text shows, Boëthius considered music proper as the theoretical side, not the practical aspect.

How much more splendid is the knowledge of music based on workmanship and effect; by as much as mind surpasses body....Thus, a musician is the man who has acquired a knowledge of music by theory--not by slavish submission to the work, but by the rule of reason. All that is set in theory and reasoning will properly be assigned to music.[57]

Music, for Boëthius, is best understood from a rational standpoint, not from that of practice. The true musician is the man who engages in the science of music, not to perform it, but from a purely speculative interest. Boëthius even praises Pythagoras for dealing with music without ever having recourse to hearing.[58]

Boëthius' fundamental attitude is a mixture of neo-Platonic thought regarding the ethical consequences of music and Pythagorean in its mathematical element.

Music is number made audible. Sound is motion (rhythm).
Motion is made up of parts (vibrations).

> Whence it follows that all sound is seen to
> consist of certain parts. But every
> conjunction of parts is put together through
> a certain proportion. Therefore the
> conjunction of sounds is organized and
> regulated through proportion. Proportions
> are primarily considered in numbers.[59]

Indeed, this sonorous concept can be expanded to the
notion that beauty is numerical, and this is exactly
what Boëthius does: "beauty appears to be a certain
commensurateness of parts."[60] Music as number, beauty
as proportion of parts--one does not have to go far in
cosmologizing these ideas and depicting the beauty and
perfection in God's universe in musico-mathematical
terms. At this juncture, Boëthius placed music in the
mainstream of Medieval philosophy. Music becomes a
microcosm of the macrocosm as it reflects universal
order through its numerical relationships--all without
reference to heard music.

Like his forerunners, Boëthius systematically
divides music into theory and practice.[61] The theoretical side of the dyad is further divided: musica mundana
and musica humana. The practical component is called
musica instrumentalis. Musica mundana is the music of
the spheres, it is the numerical harmony of the motions
of the planets and stars. It is also the harmony of
the eternal progress of the seasons. The music that is
created by these harmonious fittings-together is

unheard, except by the human soul, and thus is the
highest form of music in view of its discarnate state.
Musica humana is both physical and spiritual. There is
a harmony of our bodily parts called good health. There
is also an harmonious, or so one can hope, relationship
between body and soul. These create music which is a
relationship of parts which can be represented numerically. The lowest form of music is musica instrumentalis. This sounding music is both vocal and instrumental as Boëthius sees the human voice as an instrument. The sole purpose of aural music is the concrete
demonstration of mathematical ratios. All instrumental
music is derived from the speculative thought of "musicians." This brings us to the point, to be carried on
by later writers, that the musician (musicus) is the
theorist, and he who performs is a cantor, not a musician.

The importance and influence of Boëthius' De Inst.
Mus. should not be underestimated. Not only did he give
to the Middle Ages Greek harmonic thought, through this
work and others he solidified the quadrivium. The term
itself is Boëthius'; he introduces it in De Institutione
Arithmetica (I, 1). Bower claims that "this is the
origin of the term in Western education, as well as one
of the primary sources for the very concept."[62]
Medieval education was grounded in the study of the
quadrivium and the trivium (grammar, rhetoric and dialectic) as they were presented by Boëthius.

The De Inst. Mus. is the most thorough study of
music to come out of the early Middle Ages and was
widely read and used as the source for ancient thought.

The popularity of this work is shown by the existence of
at least 82 surviving manuscript copies of the work.[63]
Along with the great number of copies of this work that
must have existed, the very name "Boëthius" held as much
authority as the work itself. If a notion was shown to
be Boëthian, then it must be correct. In our survey of
Medieval music treatises this authority will be amply
demonstrated. Boëthius is cited as an authority more
than any other musical theorist, thus transmitting the
musical ideas of Ptolemy, Aristoxenus and Aristotle to
the writers of the next millennium. It is safe to say
that the mathematical concept of music inherited from
the Greeks by Boëthius and passed to the Middle Ages and
thus to us still exerts tremendous influence on music
theory qua mathematical science.

4. Cassiodorus, 485-575

Flavius Magnus Aurelius Cassiodorus Senator wrote a
chapter on music in his compendium De Artibus ac
Disciplinis Liberalium Litterarum.[64] Compared to St.
Augustine and Boëthius, this contribution is a trifle
covering only 4 1/2 columns in Migne's edition.
Cassiodorus relies heavily for his musical knowledge on
the works of the Pythagoreans, Ptolemy, Martianus
Capella, Aristides Quintilianus, and others.

Cassiodorus conceives of music in the wide ancient
meaning of the term: "music is diffused through all the
actions of our life." Our minds and bodies obey
harmonic laws laid down by the Creator.[65] He defines
music much in the same way as St. Augustine: "the

knowledge of apt modulation." Music, in general, is
honed down to musical science and mathematics, as he
puts it: "Musica est disciplina vel scientia quae de
numeris loquitur."[66] Under this general rubric music is
divided into harmonics, rhythmics and metrics all
grounded theoretically with no mention of musical
practice.

The nearest Cassiodorus comes to writing about
musical practice is a short discussion about musical
instruments. In § 6 of his De Musica he gives us
three of the traditional divisions of musical instruments: idiophones; chordophones; and aereophones. He
leaves out of this short discussion membranophones
(stretched-skin instruments) and, of course, electrophones. His nomenclature is: "There are three classes
of musical instruments: instruments of percussion,
instruments of tension, wind instruments." He goes on
to give a description of each class. Instruments of
percussion are metal instruments that "when struck,
yield an agreeable clanging." Instruments of tension
are constructed with strings, e.g., kithare. "Wind
instruments are those which are actuated to produce a
vocal sound when filled by a stream of air," e.g.,
trumpets, organs, etc.[67] The remainder of the work is
an harmonic exposition drawn from Gaudentius'
Eisagoge.[68] Cassiodorus ends his musical exposition
with the virtues of the "keys" and mentions the harmony
of the spheres.

As an encyclopedist Cassiodorus was widely read and
used in Medieval education. Thus, this short essay on

music was also known and quoted by subsequent writers on
music.

5. Isidore of Seville, 560-636

Isidore of Seville, another encyclopedist, wrote a
twenty-book compendium called the Etymologiae.[69] This
work contains information about the seven liberal arts,
much biblical exegesis, facts about fabulous monsters,
stones, war, furniture and some scant pages about music.
In a word, they are Cassiodorus revisited, the
difference here being that each subject is treated from
the standpoint of the origin of its technical terms.

Like St. Augustine and Cassiodorus, Isidore tells
us that music is the art of modulation (modulationis),
and takes its name from the muses (apo tou musthai)
which he says means to inquire into the power of
sound.[70] It is said that many of his etymologies are
fanciful.

One of the first statements in this work is a
negative one about notation <§ 15>. Isidore states
that unless sounds are remembered they are lost "for
they cannot be written down." Musical notation at this
time was a system of stenographic symbols showing
melodic contour, but not showing accurate pitches or
rhythm. All this must be preserved in memory. We are
going to find that the expanse that exists at this time
between theory and practice will become bridged as the
art of musical notation grows and becomes capable of
recording the size of intervals and duration. What

singers and instrumentalists were doing could then be written down. However, in the 6th century accurate notation was a theorist's fantasy.

Regarding the divisions of music, Isidore follows Cassiodorus' divisions into harmonics, rhythmics and metrics <§ 18>. On the practical side, Isidore does discuss musical instruments (organology) and gives some of their characteristics, e.g., "the sambuca, among musicians, is a kind of drum. The word means a kind of fragile wood, from which tibiae are made" <§ 11>.[71] In reality, the sambuca, from the Greek sambuke, was a kind of stringed instrument which has come down to us as the hurdy-gurdy.

Of greater interest is § 23 "Of Musical Numbers." It is noteworthy not only for its brevity, fifteen lines, but also for its mistakes stemming from a misreading of Boëthius.[72] Isidore relates to us the method for obtaining the harmonic mean between two numerical extremes (he chooses the weights of two of Pythagoras' hammers):

> say 6 and 12, you see by how many units 12
> exceeds 6, and it is by 6 units. You square
> this: 6 times 6 is 36. You then add
> together those first extremes, 6 and 12;
> together they make 18. You then divide 36 by
> 18, which gives 2. Add this to the smaller
> number, that is, 6; this will give you 8, and
> it will be the harmonic mean between 6 and
> 12.

This method will work well and good, except that it
works only if the greater extreme is twice the lesser.
Isidore's mistake is in squaring the difference; it
should be multiplied by the lesser term.[73] Of course,
this has nothing to do with musical practice. Nevertheless, Isidore does write about the correct use of hymns,
antiphons, laudes, etc., in another work on the Divine
Office.[74]

The importance of the Etymologiae lies in its
encyclopedic nature and in that it was considered a
sine qua non in every monastic library.

To sum up these early Medievalists: we have seen
that these writers inherited from the Greeks a penchant
for mathematizing music. In some instances, they took
that mathematization and engaged in cosmological flights
of fancy. Ethics and virtue were still seen to be
influenced and agitated musically. Nevertheless, these
mental acrobatics were still no reflection of what performers were doing. One possible reason for this dis-
parity was the lack of an adequate notation system for
preserving a record of interval size, durations and
hints at interpretation. As Isidore wrote: all must be
remembered, or it will be lost. As long as music theorists and composers were unable to write down what
practical musicians were doing, there was no accurate
way for them to attempt verbal descriptions. Besides,
mathematics offered an outlet for speculation, and the
weight of ancient tradition obviated verbal descriptions
of contemporaneous music.

Nevertheless, the 8th century did see the
beginnings of the use of neumes as notational signs.
These neumes (Gk: pneuma) would eventually evolve into
shaped notes that would become the notation of the
common practice period (1650-1900) that is still standard today. Most scholars believe that these notational
devices were an outgrowth of the accent signs used in
Greek and are an indication of voice inflection: a
rising sign / indicates a rise in pitch and a descending
slash \ a lowering of pitch. Combining these two signs
eventually led to neumes for two or more notes. Later on
(13th and 14th centuries) these neumes acquired note heads
to indicate duration and a staff to indicate fixed pitches
and interval sizes.

6. St. Odo of Cluny, 878-942

Seven works have come down to us under the supposed
authorship of Odo of Cluny. They range from a dialogue
on music, a tonary, a short work on arithmetic, to a
work on organ pipe scales. The two works that speak to
our project are Dialogus de Musica and the Tonarius.[75]
Even though manuscripts of the dialogue bear Odo's name,
three facts suggest that he is not the author. First,
in the Dialogus de Musica, Odo is cited as having
emended the antiphon O beatum pontificem.[76] The
question arises: Would Odo have referred to himself in
the third person in a work that he wrote? Second, a
biography of Odo was written by his contemporary John of
Salerno. This biography mentions Odo's writings, but
does not mention a dialogue on music.[77] Lastly, such a
dialogue did not survive in the library at Cluny, which

was meticulously kept through the 12th century.
Abhorring the euphony of the pseudo-Odo and realizing
the doubtfulness of the authorship of these works, I
will, in the following pages, regard Odo as the actual
perpetrator. As Sitwell writes in his translation of
John's biography: "Rightly or wrongly Odo has his place
in the history of music."[78]

There are twelve extant manuscript copies of a
Dialogus de Musica which bear Odo of Cluny's name. The
one which I will examine is printed in Gerbert and its
provenance is Paris.[79] The dialogue is preceded by a
prologue, as are eight other manuscripts of the work.
In this prologue Odo explains his purpose, which is to
"communicate to you a few rules concerning music, these
to be only of a sort which boys and simple persons may
understand ... to perfect skill in singing."[80] From the
very beginning we know that this is a pedagogical work on
the way Odo taught "actual boys and youths" how to sing.

The impetus behind this endeavor was Odo's
dissatisfaction with the state of the art of singing in
the 10th century, and this dialogue offers a corrective.
He tells us that melodies have been corrupted by
unskilled singers and that "we found sounds belonging to
the high modes and excessive ascents and descents
<singing wrong intervals>, contrary to the rules" being
performed.[81] Odo proposes to teach this science of
music through a notation system and the concomitant
sounds on the monochord. This instrument can show the
singer the exact interval to be sung so that there will
be no "excessive ascents and descents" in his singing.
What a tremendous breakthrough were the notational

symbols that correspond to musical sounds. Such had not
been attempted since the ancients.

Odonian notation consists of letters for the
pitches, such as the ancients had used. But an important advance was the use of lower-case letters for the
repeated gamut. The following is an example of Odo's
notation, which is transcribed neumatically by
Strunk:[82]

E   F   E   G   a c c
Haec est,   quae nescivit

Ex. 1. Odonian notation

Odo goes on to describe in detail the modal system
(chaps 6-18) in which he defines mode or tonus <u>modus
vel tonus</u> as "a rule which classes every melody
according to its final."[83] I must note in passing that
Odo writes of modes in melodic terms, <u>not</u> scalar terms.
Chapters 11-18 give the specific characteristics of each
mode and examples of chants in these modes.

The other musical work said to be Odo's is a
tonary.[84] Like all tonaries, Odo's is practical in that
it provides a basis for learning chant. One curious
aspect of the copy that is in Gerbert is the pitch
nomenclature used. Odo writes:

> Secunda differentia inchoat in quarta chorda, quae
> vocatur <u>Scembs</u>, & ascendit in sexta chorda,
> quae dicitur <u>neth</u>, & descendit ad primam,
> quae vocatur <u>bu</u>, & repausa ubi incipit.[85]

Michel Huglo, in his Les Tonaires, offers the
explanation that these syllables outline enechemata
(nonnanoeane).[86] Even if this be the case, it does not
explain the odd pitch names. Haggh, in his commentary
to Riemann's History of Music Theory, discusses a
possible source for this pitch nomenclature.

> The "barbaric tone-names" have a Semitic
> appearance and some are even identifiable as
> being of Arabic derivation. Scemb, Cemar,
> Asel, and Nar are Arabian names for Sun,
> Moon, Saturn, and Fire.[87]

Farmer, in his article on Islamic music in the New
Oxford History of Music, further explains these pitch
names as a reflection of the ethos of the Islamic
melodic modes and the Syrian oktoechoi.[88] At least in
name only we have a vague connection in Odo with ancient
cosmologies. Farmer also suggests that Odo's source
might possibly be from some Arabic source such as al-
Kindi (803-873 BC) who wrote several books on music.[89]
Even though it is highly speculative, it is within the
realm of possibility that the common source for Greek
letter notation and Odonian letter notation lies buried
in an Oriental past. At least it is a point for reflection that al-Kindi certainly, and possibly Pythagoras as
well, lived and studied in Baghdad.

In conclusion, the importance for our project of
Odo's musical writings is twofold. The Dialogue is the
first extant practical musical treatise as opposed to
the bevy of theoretical works we have seen. This is
why, in some manuscripts, the dialogue is subtitled

"Musica Enchiridionis," i.e., musical handbook. With so
many other music books that we have looked at, numerous
authors are mentioned as sources. Not so with Odo,
because he had no sources for the practical side of his
musical writings. We have seen the possibility of an
Arabian source for the smattering of theory contained in
the Tonarius. Secondly, we have the beginnings of a
musical notation. Odo's notation begins a long
struggle, which is not over yet, to describe adequately
on paper the parameters of musical performance. Isidore
of Seville lamented that all must be remembered, or it
will be lost; Odo has turned the tide that will bring
music theory and music practice closer together.

7. Guido d'Arezzo, 995-1050

In the prologue to an antiphoner, Guido wrote:
"...when the service is celebrated it often sounds, not
as if we were praising God, but as if we were having a
quarrel."[90] In order to rectify this noisy situation,
Guido wrote several practical musical handbooks teaching
singers how to sing and even compose. There are four
works that have come down to us from Guido's hand: the
Micrologus;[91] the prologue to an antiphoner mentioned
above; a verse-introduction to another antiphoner called
Regulae Rhythmicae;[92] and, a letter to a friend, Brother
Michael, known as Epistola de ignoto cantu.[93]

By far the most important of these works is the
Micrologus. It became the practical, as opposed to
theoretical, music teacher for the remainder of the

Middle Ages. The popularity of the work is attested to
by the existence of at least 77 manuscript copies.

In the Micrologus Guido introduces a pitch nomenclature as a singing aid, using letters of the alphabet
much like Odo's notation. Guido thought that he was
following Boëthius in using a seven-letter notation.[94]
Where Odo's gamut contained 15 steps, Guido extends this
to 21 steps.[95] The notation of this gamut, coupled
with using the monochord to learn intervals, was a great
help in singing unfamiliar music. Another invention of
Guido (at least later theorists attributed it to him) is
the Guidonian hand which was used as a singing aid.
Each pitch of the gamut has its place on the open palm
of the hand, and by pointing to the proper place on the
palm, a chant could be sung by a choir.

Another innovation of Guido is the musical staff.
This comes in his Regulae de ignoto cantu (p. 35b) where
he describes a three- or four-line staff upon which the
neumes used in his day could be drawn. Each line would
represent a fixed pitch whose letter name would be
placed at the beginning of the line. When a neume would
fall on a line it would take the pitch of the line. A
forerunner of this staff can be found in the 9th-century
anonymous handbook, Musica Enchiriadis, where one line
is used to represent a fixed pitch.

Guido also gives us a method by which we may
compose chant lines.[96] The method is really quite
simple and one can compose passable chant by using it.
First, lay out the gamut in the following manner:

Second, place the vowels, starting with whichever one
you desire, under each consecutive pitch and follow in
order. Third, since any text one may choose will have
combinations of only five vowels, choose a particular
five-note section of the gamut to be used as melody
source. Lastly, lay out the text in syllabic form and
match vowel for pitch as in the example below. What we
have in this method is a kind of proto-serialism.

Ex. 2. A Guidonian Melody

One of the most important chapters in the
Micrologus, at least for the history of counterpoint, is
the chapter on the principles of organum.[97]
Tatarkiewicz, in his History of Aesthetics, claims that
the introduction of counterpoint was the greatest
revolution in the history of music.[98] Counterpoint had
already been introduced in the Musica Enchiriadis of the
late 9th century, where musical writing was notated in
terms of parallel 4ths and 5ths and octaves. Guido

improves upon this parallel practice by introducing
oblique motion and achieves cadences by moving through
the 3rd and 2nd to the unison.

    Guido also devised a solmization method which can
be found in the letter to Brother Michael. Guido chose
the chant melody Ut queant laxis as his starting point,
because as he writes to Brother Michael: "Do you not
see how in this melody, the six phrases begin each with
a different note?"99   These different notes form the
first six notes of the C scale as the example below
demonstrates.

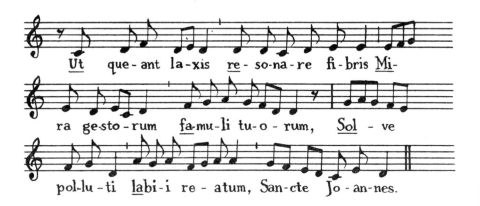

Ut que-ant la-xis re - so-na-re fi-bris Mi-

ra ge-sto-rum fa-mu-li tu-o-rum, Sol - ve

pol-lu -ti labi-i re - atum, San-cte Jo - an-nes.

Ex. 3. Ut queant laxis

The syllables of this text become a mnemonic device for
teaching new melodies and remembering intervals: ut,
re, mi, fa, sol, and la. Except for ut, which has been
replaced by the more singable do, this method is still
used today in teaching sightsinging.

Guido's work is, for the most part, practical, and
he does not seem to have depended heavily on his
predecessors for ideas, probably because enchiridia were
still rare. He does, however, end the Micrologus[100]
with the story of the Pythagorean hammers which he takes
from "the expositor of this science" Boëthius. Chapter
14 of the Micrologus has a digression on the power of
music to heal the psychologically ill. This story is
similar to one found in Cassiodorus.[101] These are the
only meeting points with the past, but this is not to be
wondered at; Guido is writing a practical musical
treatise, not a music theory. One can only speculate as
to their inclusion. Was it to lend an air of
authenticity to the handbook by mentioning ancient
authors? Was it to impress his readers with his
knowledge of music theory? Whatever the answer be,
Guido added much to the practice of music and the
eventual rapprochement of music theory and practice.

c. Gothic

It seems appropriate at this point in our project
to subdivide the Middle Ages and call the time from the
12th century down to the Renaissance the Gothic. Two
extremely important musical events, the introduction of
multi-voiced writing and the rapid advances in notation,
especially the notation of duration, speak to a change
in European musical life. The time of the School of
Notre Dame is the time of the building of the Gothic
churches in France and music seemed to go along with
these architectural changes and move toward a trans-
parent luminosity. These musical changes were so

far-reaching that they drew forth the wrath of Pope John
XXII in the Bull of 1324, in which he condemns the production of new melodies and was horrified at the disdain
shown toward the basic principles of traditional Church
music. Let us now examine three musicologists, one of
whom was also a composer, and chronicle the rise of this
tradition-shattering music.

1.   John of Garland, 1195-_c_. 1271

The two works on music which concern us are De
Plana Musica[102] and De Mensurabili Musica.[103] Before we
launch into John's contributions to musicology it must
be noted that a controversy has smoldered for years as
to how many Johns of Garland there were and who wrote
what. William Waite has, to some degree, snuffed out
this quarrel in his demonstration that the two Johns are
actually one.[104] However this may be, our concern is
with the works and not with John's bilocation.

The De Plana Musica exists in three manuscript
sources,[105] the most notable of which wound up as the
first thirteen chapters of Philippe de Vitry's Ars Nova.
In this work John tells us that there are three
varieties of music, mundana, humana and instrumentalis,
and that his concern will be with the last of the
three.[106] He continues to divide and subdivide his
subject to the point that he is only concerned with the
diatonic, not chromatic nor enharmonic, in which he
posits the 13 intervals of music. This is one of the
first theoretical discussions of these intervals.[107] He
gives all the numerical proportions of these intervals

and then applies them to the monochord, which can be
seen as a movement from the theoretical to the practical
side of music. As a matter of fact, John admonishes his
readers in chapter 10 on mutations, that if they would
better understand the theory, "let them look again at
the monochord." Chapter 11 gives us a definition of
music that has moved completely away from the speculation and mathematics of an earlier period to a practical
one:

> Observe that music is the knowledge of
> accurate singing, or <vel> an easy means of
> achieving perfection in singing. And its
> name is derived from moys, which is water,
> and ycos, knowledge, because it was invented
> according to water.[108]

While the De Plana Musica deals with unmeasured music,
i.e., plainchant, the De Mensurabili Musica deals with
measured music, which John calls organum in the generic
sense.[109] In the course of this work John addresses
himself to several musical problems: rhythmic notation;
notation in general; classification of intervals; and a
description of three styles of contemporary counterpoint: discant, copula, and organum. The first eight
chapters deal with the rhythm and notation in all six
rhythmic modes. It is in this section that John's
interests in rhetoric and poetry are most evident.
John's notational innovations were of such importance
that they were carried on by his successors, as Franco
of Cologne adopted John's method of denoting the duration of rests, which he defines as a "cessation of sound
made in a proper quantity."[110] John also introduced a

graphic method of distinguishing between single notes
of the same species, e.g., duplex long and the plicated
long, etc.; in his De Mensurabili Musica he gives many
one-line examples of this device, e.g., the duplex long
as ▉▉▉ , the semibreve as ◆◆◆ , etc.[111] One of the
most important innovations was his introduction of the
concept of propriety and perfection in ligatures.[112]

Chapters 9 and 10 are concerned with the
classification of musical intervals, i.e., "consonances
sounded at the same time."[113] John, unlike any of his
predecessors, gives a full explanation of all 13 intervals from the unison to the octave. In the course of
his discussion he defines consonance, what he calls a
concord: "two sounds joined at the same time so that
one can be heard as compatible with the other." He also
tells us what a dissonance, i.e., discord, is when these
two sounds "cannot be heard as compatible with each
other."[114] It has not been since Aristoxenus that a
musicologist has had recourse to the ears in determining
the nature of musical sound. John's nomenclature for
these intervals, which he inherited from Boëthius, is
Greek. Chapter 10 also deals with the mathematical
proportions that exist between intervals, and his exposition is thoroughly Pythagorean, without mentioning the
Ionian. One aspect of John's writing about intervals is
his treatment of the nature of the 3rd. (This will
become increasingly important, especially in the Renaissance.) Thirds having, since antiquity, been considered
a discord, John is innovative in calling both the major
and minor thirds concords, albeit imperfect. The nature
of this imperfection is that "when two sounds appear
together at the same time so that the ears can wholly

distinguish one voice from the other" they are
imperfect.[115]

The remainder of the _De Mensurabili Musica_ is
devoted to counterpoint and its three species: discant,
copula and organum. In this section on counterpoint,
John describes all the possible combinations, in two
voices, of the six modes. His explanation constitutes
one of the first full accounts of counterpoint. Indeed,
as Birnbaum points out in an appendix to his translation, John goes beyond the bounds of a description of
practice into _musica speculativa_:

> This classification is a theoretical system
> which is used only as a convenient means for
> providing examples of the various
> possibilities in discant compositions;
> Garlandia's scheme has little relevance to
> the music or its notation.[116]

John of Garland's importance lies in several
directions, without which subsequent music history would
have been different. He was the first to systematize
fully the rhythmic modes and their notation--indeed he
systematized them right into speculation. He gave a
full explanation of the relationships between the 13
intervals and espoused a doctrine of consonance and
dissonance that remained unchanged to the mid-1500's.
Subsequent medieval polyphony would not have been
possible without John of Garland. As we shall see, none
other than Franco of Cologne incorporated whole sections
of John's musical writings into his _Ars Cantus
Mensurabilis_.

2. Franco of Cologne, fl. 1250-1280

Borrowing abundantly from the past and making
innovations which are still part of common practice
notation, Franco wrote his Ars Cantus Mensurabilis some-
where around the year 1260.[117] The work is a practical
exposition of 13th-century part-writing and an explanation of notational practices with several improvements.
Although the text is practical in nature, Franco does
mention one speculative theorist as having laid the
foundation, at least theoretically, for plainsong, that
being Boëthius. On the practical plainsong side, Franco
mentions Guido as having fully explained plainsong from
that aspect.[118] This is Franco's nod to the past in
which he distinguishes between theory and practice. He
then launches into his description of 13th-century music.

His major contributions are threefold. First, he
reclassified the rhythmic modes and reduced them from
six or seven to five modes,[119] thus simplifying the
system. Second, he attached definite durations to
definite note-shapes.[120] In the past there were other
factors that signified duration other than the shape of
the notes, e.g., the numerical position in a series of
ligatures. Lastly, he fully codified the system of
rests as given in John of Garland.[121] Gustave Reese
sums up Franco's importance for future generations:

> Franco's system survived with most of its
> essential features intact, but with important
> accretions, into the 16th century, and, how-
> ever far we may have travelled from it
> <Franconian notation> in details in almost

seven centuries still provides the fundamental principles upon which our own notation
is based.[122]

3.   Philippe de Vitry, 1291-1361

The refinement of mensural notation went forward at
the hands of the Bishop of Meaux. As a musician
Philippe wrote music and an authoritative treatise on
musical practice, Ars Nova (1320).[123] There are four
extant copies of this work, two in France, one in
England and one at the Vatican. As was stated in the
section on John of Garland, the first 13 chapters are
most likely not by Vitry and those that remain vary so
much in the manuscripts that some scholars believe them
to be the compilation of several students of Vitry.[124]

Vitry's contributions lie mainly in solving more
problems in mensural notation. His innovations deal
mostly with problems of rhythm and the notation of
duration. He was the first to recognize, without
theological and philosophical speculation, the equal
importance and status of perfect (triple time) and
imperfect (duple time) mensuration. He also discusses
the variations possible in these two times. To show
which type of mensuration was meant in a piece, he
introduced the idea of the time signature, e.g., a
circle for perfect and a half-circle (which we still
use) for imperfect time.[125] Another device he introduced that we still use is the dotted note to indicate
an addition of temporal length to the value of the note.
It was also used as a means of dividing groups of notes

from each other. The "dot" was introduced in his music;
it was not mentioned in the Ars Nova.

Chapter 19 of this work deals with another
invention of the Bishop: "De notulis rubeis," red
notes. Since it is now possible to compose in perfect
and imperfect time, some means was needed to tell the
performer when to change from perfect to imperfect time
and vice versa. Vitry introduced red notes, later
white, to show this change: three black notes are equal
to two red notes. Red notes could also be used "to
indicate that they are sung an octave from the pitch at
which they appear." Also, "red notes are used to
differentiate the proper chant" from those notes that do
not belong to the chant melody.[126] Vitry is also
credited with introducing the minim (half-note) as a
note form.

A compositional process that is characteristic of
the Ars Nova is that used in writing isorhythmic motets.
These motets were composed using a structural principle
which repeats a schema of time values, called the talea,
in presenting a liturgical melody or cantus firmus,
called color; usually this line is the tenor. This
isorythmic line then is cantus firmus over which are
composed the added parts of the motet. It must be noted
that the isorhythmic, i.e., same-duration pattern,
nature of these tenors is not heard, it is an organi-
zational principle.[127]

All of these innovations, some by Vitry, and others
by his contemporaries, were so new and radical and
opposed to the traditions of the ars antiqua that, as

mentioned earlier, Pope John XXII, in the Bull of 1324, condemned this new school for writing new melodies that went against the musical laws of the church and the ancients and whose sole purpose was to intoxicate the ear.[128] The text of this Bull does offer one major problem: it is difficult to decide if the Pope is condemning the practice of composers or the practice of performers, which might have been rather different from what composers were notating. Nevertheless, Vitry's advancements had tremendous influence on practical music. The systematization and solution to problems in the notation of duration coupled with the equalization of duple and triple time gave composers a graphic freedom they had never possessed. These new rhythmic freedoms and continued contrapuntal experimentations gave rise to new art forms which would reach complexities never dreamed of by Franco or John of Garland.

In summation: including the Gothic, the great amount of time covered by the Middle Ages, from the 4th to the 14th centuries, saw three major changes in the relationship and importance between speculative or theoretical and practical musical writings.

First, the shift away from musical theory in the style of the ancients was first made by Odo of Cluny. His was a desire to perfect the singing of "boys and simple persons." He introduced a notation to aid in this endeavor. Nearly every subsequent music treatise was practical in nature, although some of them contained theoretical matters, e.g., John of Garland's codification of the rhythmic modes.

Second, and going hand-in-hand with the handbook on
music, are the increasing attempts at notating what
people do when they make music. Isidore of Seville had
lamented the lack of a notation--his dream came true
nine centuries later. Many attempts were made to solve
the problem of notating pitch and its location in the
gamut plus the nightmare of notating duration. Pitch
and intervals came first with the introduction of
letters for pitches. Actually, this was a reintroduction, as the Greeks had used a letter notation. From
the Musica Enchiriadis (ca. 900)[129] we get daseian notation, which uses the symbol for a rough breathing from
Greek plus the letters S, C and C-reversed. These
compound symbols were presented in all possible posi-
tions to represent pitches. The symbols plus a text
were presented on a primordial staff. Hermannus
Contractus (1013-1054) devised a system of notation
which used letters to indicate intervals, e.g.,
e=unison, s=semitone, d=4th, etc. Again we are tied to
the text for rhythm and the duration of individual
pitches. Neumes were also invented as stenographic
symbols which outline the shape of a melody but do not
indicate duration. These were basically a mnemonic
device for learning chants. Finally, in the 11th
century, these neumes developed into the square shape
and were put on lines to indicate pitch level. These
lines were originally colored to indicate pitch level.
By the end of the Gothic period all the major problems
attendant upon the notation of music had been solved
with the innovations of Franco of Cologne and Philippe
de Vitry.

Lastly, counterpoint, as Tatarkiewicz writes, "was one of the greatest revolutions in the history of music."[130] Counterpoint is the simultaneous sounding of two or more voices at different pitch levels. The Musica Enchiriadis contains two-part organa which constitute some of the earliest examples of notated counterpoint. From these beginnings the whole fabric of Western music has been woven. One of the major fundamental characteristics of Western music is this concept of layers of melodies, which began as these 10th-century organa.

Speculative music theory did not die out with the onslaught of music handbooks and notation guides; it moved into the arena of the philosopher-theologians who kept alive the ancient concepts about music and cosmic harmony. The tradition of the Pythagoreans handed down through Plato's Timaeus was alive in the Middle Ages. As has been noted earlier, John Scotus Eriugena wrote in the 9th century that the beauty and harmony in music is in its ability to speak to the inner soul and not the sounds themselves.[131]

d. Renaissance

So much has been written on the relationship between the Middle Ages and the Renaissance: when one begins and the other ends; the general similarities and differences between the two; that I propose not to spill any more ink on the subject. There are Medieval characteristics vis-à-vis theory and practice that flow right through the Renaissance, e.g., Pythagorean cosmology.

One suddenly becomes aware of a change, but is hard
pressed to say when the change began. Theory, for the
most part, is just a reintroduction and reinforcement of
ancient music theory that had gone underground in the
late Middle Ages, which was overrun with isagoges.
Music theory reëmerges to reinforce the musical practices of the Gothic Netherlands School of the 15th
century.

     Renaissance musicologists effected a synthesis
between ancient and early Medieval theory and late
Medieval musica practica which started around the time
of Odo of Cluny. This synthesis was to become the
systematic half of musicology as codified by Guido Adler
in the 19th century. It is also possible to see the
introductions to many of the Renaissance treatises that
we will peruse, in which antique and Medieval musical
knowledge is reviewed, as being "historical" in nature.
This could be seen as the first attempts at historical
musicology, but more of that later.

     On the theoretical or speculative side of this
duality, Renaissance theorists accepted the main tenets
of music theory as espoused by the Ancients and Medieval
musicologists. Music is a science like geometry and
arithmetic. Music is not confined to the audible world,
but speaks to the human soul. Composers simply copy the
harmonious relationships that exist in the cosmos and
the true musician is the one who ratiocinates about this
phenomenon. Different harmonies have their psychological effect upon us and can cause moral uplift or decay.

This theory was coupled with a humanist's interests
in man and the composer, i.e., the practical side of
music, and produced a universal musical concept
embracing both the speculative and the practical. Let
us now look closer at four musicologists from this
epoch.

1. Johannes Tinctoris, c. 1435-1511

Tinctoris was a Franco-Flemish theorist and
composer whose twelve works on music can be divided into
five distinct groups: dictionary; music and ethics,
therapy, etc.; mensural notation; practical music; and,
the art of writing music. There are three outstanding
works at which we need to look closely in order to gain
an understanding of Tinctoris as a musicologist:
Terminorum Musicae Diffinitorium (1472);[132] De
Inventione et Usu Musicae (1480);[133] and, Liber de Arte
Contrapuncti (1477).[134]

The Diffinitorium is the first printed music
dictionary (there is an 11th century manuscript that
contains a 62-entry Vocabularium Musicum) and contains
299 definitions of basic musical terms covering both
plain chant and musica mensurabilis. In the dedication
of the dictionary, to the Princess Beatrice of Aragon,
Tinctoris tells us his purpose and the place of music in
the liberal arts which is an Ancient echo:

> Wherefore, being a student of the most
> liberal art, and the noblest among the
> mathematical arts, namely divine music, and

believing it very useful to define its terms
both in principle and in detail, by which the
things concerning it being understood, those
who practice it may the more readily grasp
its nature and its particular....[135]

To this end he gives the reader succinct
definitions of musical terms. For example, his definition of music is thoroughly practical even though he
places music in the mathematical firmament:

Music is that skill consisting of performance
in singing and playing, and it is threefold,
namely harmonic <human voice>, organal <wind
instruments>, and rhythmical <instruments
which render the sound by touch.>[136]

His definition of musician speaks to this amalgamation
of theory and practice that is a widespread Renaissance
trait:

A musician is one who takes up the metier of
singing, having observed its principles by
means of study.[137]

Here the musician is one who knows what and why he
sings. Before this, the musician was one who did not
sing but who knew.

The De Inventione et Usu Musicae is a book,
actually five books of which we have only extracts,
dealing with practical matters.[138] In the six chapters
that have come down to us Tinctoris deals with singing

in antiquity and his own day in which he mentions
singers he considers to be good.[139]   He also discusses
the history, use and manufacture of tibiae and the lyra,
which includes the viol, rebec, guitar, etc.[140]

Finally, his Liber de Arte Contrapuncti is
considered to be his most important work.   In reading
the "Prologue" to this counterpoint book one is
immediately struck by the numerous references to ancient
authors, a dearth of which was obvious in our Gothic
musicologists.   Their inclusion at this point gives
testimony to the nature of the Renaissance: an intense
interest in antiquity and an attempt to integrate
antique learning into the mainstream of Renaissance
thought.   He reiterates the harmony of the spheres in
the company of Plato, Pythagoras, Cicero, Macrobius,
Boëthius and Isidore.   Tinctoris does not hold to the
celestial harmonies as he says neither does Aristotle
nor St. Thomas Aquinas.   Harmonious sounds are brought
about by earthly instruments.   All the ancients agree,
so says Tinctoris, to this harmoniousness: Plato,
Pythagoras, Nicomachus, Aristoxenus, Philolaus,
Archytas, Ptolemy and Boëthius "but how they were
accustomed to arrange and put them <the harmonies>
together is only slightly understood at our time."
Tinctoris continues by telling us that he has held in
his hands at one time or another many old songs of
unknown authorship which are called apocrypha that are
so inept and stupidly composed that they offend our ears
rather than please them.[141]   Could he have had access to
ancient songs now lost to us?   It seems probable that
what he is talking about are certain Medieval songs that
were written down so that they could be sung and were

found to offend the ear. Also, this passage points to
the Renaissance's attitude toward the media aevum: what
the Renaissance was doing in music and the arts was so
much better than anything that went before. He even
goes so far as to say that there are those who believe
that anything written before 1435 is not "worthy of
performance."[142] The remainder of the Contrapuncti is
divided into three books: I--on consonances in simple
counterpoint; II--on dissonance; chapter 20 contains a
section on improvisation;[143] and, III--on the eight
rules of all counterpoint. These rules form the basis
for all subsequent modal-tonal counterpoint and are the
rules still taught today in that style, e.g., rule 1:
"...all counterpoint should begin and end with a perfect
consonance.[144]

     Tinctoris offers us a thoroughly humanistic
attitude toward music. His basic approach is that music
is mathematical, i.e., one can express interval
relationships numerically, but that music is not
mathematics. In him we find no cosmological or
theological speculation about musical harmony.
Tinctoris' music theory is based on constant references
to contemporary composers. Thus, his theory is
descriptive rather than speculative. This, we will
discover, is also a Renaissance trait. Tinctoris makes
reference to the works of Dunstable, Ockeghem, Busnois,
Dufay, etc. What these composers had done in practice,
Tinctoris describes in theory. One might say that
Tinctoris is an unmystical Pythagorean and is very close
to the scientific objectivity of Aristoxenus. But this
is also Renaissance in idea and concept, and we have
here the beginnings of what was to become known as the

scientific method in the 19th and 20th centuries. However, the final arbiter in music is the ear, not mathematical analysis. What the ear arbitrates, he tells us,
is the differences between consonance and dissonance,
and he defines dissonance, not in mathematical terms as
with the ancients, but as the combinations of different
sounds that are displeasing to the ear.[145]

    His concepts about the aims of music contain both
the Ancient and Medieval ideas about pleasing God and
uplifting human morality, to which he adds a humanistic
aim: giving joy to the people.[146] Whereas, with the
ancients music proper was a reflection of cosmic order
made by God and music as heard was a reflection of
cosmic harmony, Tinctoris begins to reverse this ancient
hierarchy, i.e., theory should be adapted to existing
compositions. In his dictionary, Tinctoris defines the
composer as "the creator of some new piece."[147] This
would have astonished any Medieval theorist, who would
have assumed that one worked from existing compositions,
as in the cantus firmi. The natural sciences discover
the existing universe, and composers were supposed to
discover the harmonious relationships in God's universe,
not create some new harmonies. The old order is being
turned around: a theocentric cosmology is being
replaced with an anthropocentric one. The human-
composer comes first, not the god-mathematician. Music
is becoming an art and moving away from the sciences.
This is music's Copernican revolution, and Tinctoris
helped bring it about.

2.   Pietro Aaron, c. 1480-c. 1550

This Florentine theorist and composer wrote five
treatises on music, four of which were published in
Italian. This in itself was innovative and shows a
desire to reach a wider reading public. The only work
which was published in Latin, although written in
Italian, is the Libri Tres de Institutione Harmonica
(1516).[148] This work, as the title tells us, is divided
into three books. The first book deals with plainchant.
The remaining two books deal with counterpoint and its
composition, the most important aspect of which is
Aaron's suggestion that the traditional method of
composition, line by line in the order cantus, tenor,
bass and alto, be replaced by a vertical method, that
is, simultaneously.[149] This method of composition,
vertical as opposed to horizontal, became the
Renaissance standard and has remained common to this
day. This change in compositional method reflects a
gradual change in the way composers and theorists were
thinking musically: a shift from contrapuntal to
harmonic thought.

The Toscanello de la Musica (1523), so named for
his native Tuscany, is also a treatise on counterpoint
but in more detail and with many extra-contrapuntal
ideas on music in general.[150] Aaron is advanced in his
musical thinking in favoring written indications of all
accidentals at all times--no musica ficta, the musicians' bête noire. His reason for this innovation is
simple and practical and would solve a problem that
still plagues those who perform early music: "the musician or composer is obliged to show his intention so

that the singer will not stumble into something the composer did not intend."[151] In this same work Aaron is the first theorist to explain mean-tone temperament.[152] This system of temperament was devised to correct the Pythagorean system which is quite "out" as one adds successive fifths. Aaron's system was an advance, for with mean-tone tuning it was possible to use an expanded gamut which Renaissance composers and theorists were demanding.

Like so many other Renaissance writers, Aaron's works abound in classical references as a show of erudition and to demonstrate the genesis of the art. What we get from Aaron's pen is quasi-historical in that he tells us what has happened in the past and what the present is doing with it to make it so much better. After these sometimes lengthy prolegomena, Aaron's contributions can be seen to be of a highly practical nature. Rarely does he dip into speculation. He was the first to advocate harmonic composition. He was against the practice of musica ficta, suggesting that composers write what they wanted performed. He was also one of the first to formulate a system of mean-tone temperament. Aaron's attitudes were on the whole practical--he reports what is being done musically in his own time. The fact that he wrote and published in Italian speaks to his practical nature.

3. Heinrich Glarean, 1488-1563

This Swiss humanist has left for us two musical treatises and one compendium. They are Isagoge in

Musicen (1516);[153] Dodecachordon (1547);[154] and Musicae
Epitome sive Compendium ex Glareani Dodecachordo
(1557).[155] We shall consider the first two works, as
the third is an abstract of the Dodecachordon.

The Isagoge is important, mainly because it
contains ab ovo the Dodecachordon. The work is
a handbook which he wrote to teach his boys at school.
It is an introduction to the musical art and remains at
an introductory level even though it covers a wide range
of topics. He opens with the now standard history of
the elements of music theory from Pythagoras to his own
day. He ends with the theory of scale construction,
tuning, and the Greek and Church modes. One aspect of
this Isagoge that I must share with my reader is the
personal digression that occurs in chapter VII.

In a sea of musical treatises it is refreshing to
find one in which the author allows his humanity to come
to the fore. The diatribe is so sudden and forceful
that the reader must stop and take notice. It is a
universal diatribe, one that I have heard many times:
against arrogant intellectualism, vacuous scholarship,
and the inability to say, "I don't know." Let Henry
speak for himself. After telling us the names, in
Greek, of the parts of the octave he writes:

> But even as I wrote these names, and realized
> that we are not now entirely agreed as to how
> the ancients used them and that many of the
> things that are current in our day not only
> fail to accord with them, it is not easy for
> me to put into words with what reluctance I

have wielded my pen. But there will be,
perhaps, something which I may plead in my
own behalf, that which I do not know I shall
frankly state that I do not know, a course of
action which the learned are all too loath to
pursue....What is more, if I considered
myself free to do what many have the habit of
doing, that is, to say the first thing that
comes to mind, merely to appear learned
instead of imparting learning to others in
simple good faith, I could spread a whole
forest of opinions before the studious
reader. But why carry water to the river?
It is open to anyone to talk idle nonsense,
while it falls to the few to say things truly
pertinent to the subject....the only true
musician is one who, having weighed the
evidence, acknowledges the science of song to
lie not in the bondage of practical
necessity, but under the dominion of reasoned
speculation. Little wonder that you will
find very few musicians today, for upon my
soul this bird is rarer than a white crow.
But those good disciplines which they call
liberal have deteriorated to such an extent
that by nobody are they less cultivated than
by those who make a living at them. I am
talking now about those who are commonly
called magister, or "master," who inculcate
an obscure and sophisticated reasoning in
place of the seven distinguished disciplines
about which they know scarcely a fraction,
while at the same time they gain great wealth

under the title of these same arts, although
their students go out even more stupid than
when they came in. Apparently it matters not
at all, as long as <these same "masters">
have a title or a fine crimson gown, whether
they know or do not know one whit in speech,
in learning, or even in manners from the
uncouth working man![156]

The most important contribution made in the
Dodecachordon (dodeka : twelve + chorde : string) is the
theoretical grounding and full descriptive explanation
of two additional modes which Glarean adds to the
traditional eight church modes. A glance at the title
page of the Basel edition will demonstrate the
importance Glarean placed on his modal theory. (see Ex.
4, next page) Book I of this work is a restatement of
traditional music theory based on Boëthius and
Garfurius. Glarean had edited the De Musica of Boëthius
in 1547, so he was quite conversant with the Senator's
music theory. Book II is a general discussion of 12
modes, the music theories of the ancients and monophony.
Book III deals with the same material as in II but for
polyphonic music.

The two "new" modes introduced by Glarean, the
Ionian and Aeolian with their plagals, are what will
become the major and minor tonalities that supplanted
the modal system by the mid-17th century and remained
the basic Western musical language down to the early
20th century. These "new" modes, variants of the
Lydian and Dorian, were already in use in Glarean's
time; he merely recognized them as independent modes.

GLAREANI

ΔΩΔΕΚΑΧΟΡΔΟΝ

Plagij	Authentæ
A Hypodorius	D Dorius
B Hypophrygius	E Phrygius
C Hypolydius	F Lydius
D Hypomixolyd.	G Mixolydius
E Hypoæolius	A Aeolius
G Hypoionicus	C Ionicus Porphyrio
·F Hyperphrygius	·B Hyperæolius

Hypermixolydius Ptolemæi

Hyperæolius Mar.Cap.

Hyperphrygius Mar.Cap.

Hyperiaſtius uel Hyperionicus Mar.Cap.

Hyperlydius Mart.Cap.

Hyperdorius Mart.Capell.

Hypoiaſtius Mart.Cap.

Iaſtius Apuleius & Mar.Cap.

Hyperlydius Politia. ſed eſt error

Zum Kloneaderij Bma Maria Virginis in Rottenhaſlack

BASILEÆ.

Ex. 4: Title page of Glarean's Dodecachordon

As a matter of fact, he recognized, at least in theory,
two more modes (see Ex. 4):   the Hyperaeolian (B to b)
and the Hyperphrygian (F to f).   These he rejects
because the scale cannot be divided between a perfect
5th and perfect 4th as in all the other modes.

> ...its <hyperaeolian> division has stood in
> the way, so that it has come less into use.
> For by the rule of the authentic modes it
> should have the fifth below, the fourth
> above, which is impossible in this case,
> since from ♮ to F is a diminished fifth, from
> F to mi, which is on the b key, is a
> tritone....[157]

A final important aspect of the Dodecachordon
occurs in Book III. This contains, among other material,
an anthology of contrapuntal pieces by many Dutch
masters which demonstrate and illustrate Glarean's text.
In chapter 13 Glarean describes what might be called
"harmonic relationships" in the following manner:

> There is a hidden relationship of the modes
> and a generating of one from the other,
> certainly not acquired through the ingenuity
> of symphonetae <composers>, but determined in
> this way by the nature of the modes.[158]

What Glarean is writing about could be what we call
modulation, i.e., the generation of one key area from
another because of the internal harmonic relationship
between tonic, dominant and secondary dominant tonal

areas. He could also be describing the "pull" that
exists in the relationship between different harmonies.

Glarean is an example of a Renaissance musicologist
who was conscious of his attempt at a synthesis of
ancient and modern knowledge. As with all Renaissance
humanists, he believed in the integration of the two
cultures. He goes so far as to say that the theory of
the 12-modes is not an innovation "but a proper renewal
of antiquity."[159] Glarean knew his ancient sources. He
cites 35 ancient writers in the course of the
Dodecachordon. He accepted, with the ancient authors,
the twofold division in music: theory and practice.
His theoretical definition comes from Boëthius: music
is the ability to distinguish with the senses and the
reason between different sounds. His practical definition is Augustinian: music is the science of singing
rhythmically.[160] He believes that there is an objective
harmony in the universe and that these laws are the
foundation of musica instrumentalis; however, the composer, within this natural bound, does have certain
freedom and creativity.

4. Gioseffo Zarlino, 1517-1590

The Italian musicologist Zarlino has left us three
treatises on music, one of which, Le Istitutioni
Harmoniche (1558), is the culmination of the Renaissance
synthesis of music theory and musical practice.[161] The
other two books are Sopplimenti Musicale (1558)[162] and
Dimostrationi Harmoniche (1571).[163] Not only did
Zarlino write the compendium of Renaissance music

theory, he studied composition with Adrian Willaert, and
was a composer of motets and madrigals in which he put
into practice many of his theoretical ideas, especially
concerning text underlay.[164] Zarlino was a polyglot,
fluent in Latin, Greek, and Hebrew, besides his native
Italian. He also was a student of logic and philosophy.
The gentleman was erudite and well suited to summing up
his epoch.

     Zarlino's Istitutioni is counted by most music
historians as his most important work. It is divided
into four books: I and II are traditional musica
theoretica in which he discusses the philosophical,
cosmological and mathematical basis of music, and the
Greek tonal system which he supplants with a modern
theory of consonance (into which he admits 3rds and
6ths), and tuning; book III is musical practice, i.e.,
counterpoint which is "the composition of songs of
melodies for two or more voices";[165] and book IV is his
theory of modes in which he changes the traditional
order of the modes by starting them with the Ionian (C)
and not the Dorian (D).

     Zarlino's aim in this work was to unite speculative
theory and the practice of composition, the common aim
of most Renaissance musicologists.[166] Nevertheless, he
still maintains the separation between speculation and
practice and introduces an idea that has been foreign to
music study until his time: music as an art. It is
this practical or compositional side of the traditional
dyad that has become an art for Zarlino. It is in this
area that we make judgments of taste, but these

judgments must be grounded in reason, not just
sensation. He continues:

> It is necessary that <the critic> who
> wants to judge anything pertaining to
> the art have two parts: first, that
> he be expert in things of science,
> namely, of speculation; and then also
> in those of art, which consists in
> practice.[167]

He even goes so far as to state that in order to be
able to judge music rightly one must be able to compose
music. Zarlino seems to move suddenly into the area of
pure speculation when musing on the perfect music
critic! Thus, music appeals both to the senses and to
reason, and, he says, exists for more than mere enjoyment, or else it would not have its reasonable side.
'Reason' here means that music criticism makes appeals
to science and mathematics. Music's aim is to be a
liberal art that will "guide the passions and lead the
soul towards virtue."[168]

Zarlino's importance lies in his rôle as
synthesizer of his musical heritage of ancient and
medieval theory and the musical practice of the
Renaissance. His innovations helped change the sonorous
nature of Western music from modal to tonal. He was one
of the first to recognize only two modes, major and
minor, which were to become the basic musical vocabulary
for the next 350 years. Zarlino was the starting point
for those who carried forward what was to become known
as the prima prattica into the 17th century.

The overall thrust of the four Renaissance
musicologists we have considered so far was to attempt
the integration of ancient theory and contemporary
practice. Up until this time the major writers on music
were either in the theoretical camp (up to Odo of Cluny)
or in the practical camp (from Odo through the end of
the Gothic period). With the emergent humanism and
emphasis on ancient knowledge, the writers on music in
the Renaissance attempted to bring this knowledge
together.

This does not mean that all musicologists were
intent on merging the past and the present; at least one
writer wanted to junk the present and establish a
practice based completely on what he perceived as the
Greek model. Nicola Vicentino (1511-1572) is the
musicologist of the ancients. It is in his <u>Antica
Musica</u> <u>Ridotta</u> <u>alla</u> <u>Moderna</u> <u>Prattica</u> (1555)[169] that
Nicola wants to reintroduce the chromatic and enharmonic
genera of the Greeks into mainstream Renaissance music.
He advocates the use of fifth-tones and a 31-step
division of the octave, and devised a simple notation
for these microtones:

Ex. 5. Vicentino's Microtonal Notation

The superimposed dot indicates the enharmonic genus.[170]
(The notes in brackets represent chromatic common prac-

tice notation with three notes to the whole-step.)
Nicola even constructed a keyboard instrument, called
the arcicembalo, with two keyboards and six orders of
keys upon which one could reproduce these chromatic and
enharmonic genera. Several such instruments were constructed over the years and some music written for them,
but they never caught on, at least until the 20th
century. Vicentino is often characterized as the avant-
garde theorist of the Renaissance, or so he must have
seemed to his contemporaries. From our vantage point,
his work seems to be reactionary, looking backward
instead of forward.

One cannot sail through the Renaissance, as we have
done, without mentioning Galileo Galilei and his
contributions to what will become the application of
scientific methods to the physical phenomena of musical
sound. In his work Discorsi dimonstrazioni
mathematiche, intorno à due nuove scienze (1638) he
devotes some twelve pages to music.[171] In these pages
Galileo is concerned with an explanation of the nature
of consonance and dissonance. He offers two accounts of
the phenomena: physical and physiological. The
physical explanation is based on string lengths and
mathematics (proportions) but also on the phenomenon of
overtones. His physiological explanation turns on the
concordant or discordant movement of ear cartilage
depending upon the interval and frequency of the sound.

The most important aspect of Galileo's musical
excursus is his mathematization of nature. Musical
intervals, being a sound phenomenon, are part of nature,
and were seen, in the Greek tradition, as mathematical

ratios. Galileo took these mathematical ratios and
expanded them into acoustical laws governing a natural
phenomenon. We see here a scientific process, experimentation and induction, that is to gain more and more
ground in the next centuries and ultimately be the
methodological aspiration of a nascent musicology in
the 19th century.

Three writers, who were non-musicians, must be
mentioned before we quit the Renaissance. Giorgio
Valla's encyclopedia De expetendis et fugiendis rebus
(101) contains five sections on music, all based on a
highly rationalistic neo-Pythagoreanism. He, like
Vicentino, wanted a reinstatement of Greek theory and
wanted to construct a chordoton which would yield the
disdiapason. Faber Stapulensis, in his De musica menta
musicalia (1496), was more concerned with the ethical
nature of ancient music. He felt that Boëthius had
given that ethos to the West, but it had been lost.
This was a common feeling among Renaissance humanists,
that modern music was inferior to ancient music because
it possessed no distinctive ethos. Lastly, we must
mention Marsilio Ficino and his De rationibus Musicae
(1484). Ficino, along with Cosimo d'Medici and
Gemisthus Pletho, was the founder of the Florentine
Academy dedicated to the translation and dissemination
of Platonic thought. Marsilio's musical writings were
firmly based on his Hellenistic-Plotinian exegesis of
Plato--all beauty and art is grounded in the harmony
of the universe.

Finally, the first glimmers of an historical
attitude towards music can be seen in our Renaissance

musicologists. Each of them recites for us a catalog of
ancient music theory upon which they want to ground and
augment Renaissance practice. This is not history for
the sake of history, but history for the sake of musical
practice. These writers felt a direct line of descent
from the Greeks, and there is a sense of a causal
relationship between, e.g., Greek modal theory and that
of the 16th century. One never gets the feeling or sense
that Glarean is writing about Greek theory simply because
it is fascinating; as a matter of fact he tells us that
nobody really knows what he is talking about when it
comes to Greek music; it is merely something to be
used to explain why music is the way it is, and the
present age could do so much more than the past, if
only one liberated oneself from the ancient and classical
models.

Let us sum up the history of this musical
bifurcation started by the ancients. The Pythagoreans
mathematized musical intervals in the service of a
cosmology. Even though this mathematization was from
heard, not imagined, sound it was not done for practical
musical purposes. Other ancient writers in this
tradition are Plato and Ptolemy. Plato, however, does
give hints of practical musical matters in the Republic
(530d-531c) but is not concerned with this side of
music. On the practical side of our dyad are the
writers Aristotle and Aristoxenus. Both of these men
are content to describe music and do not seem to put
that knowledge to extra-musical use. Thus, our ancient
writers on music used it in one of two ways: either as
an end in itself; or, in service of extra-musical
matters, e.g., cosmology.

The Middle Ages, through the writings of Boëthius
and others, continued this speculative tradition that
used music theory for extra-musical purposes. With Odo
of Cluny (10th century) we have one of the first practical musical handbooks. This interest in the practical
side of our musical dyad runs parallel to the first
attempts at the notation of current practice. From this
time to the Renaissance the majority of musical treatises are practical: teaching singing, notation and
composition. As we saw, the speculative side of the
science passed to the philosophers and theologians who
used music in the ancient manner as an explanation of
the harmony of God's creation.

Writers during the Renaissance discovered and
reintroduced ancient Greek music theory into the musical
mainstream for the purpose of explaining current musical
practices and to lend an air of authority to their
theoretical musings. The result was a fusion of ancient
theory and Renaissance practice that created what we
call music theory. This became the speculative side of
the musicological project, as we shall see, as espoused
by Guido Adler in the 19th century.

NOTES FOR CHAPTER II

[1]For a thorough study of the monochord see Cecil Adkins, "The Theory and Practice of the Monochord," Diss. University of Iowa, 1963.

[2]See the following: Nichomachus and Gaudentios in Marcus Meibom, Antiquae musicae auctores septem (Amstelodami: apud Ludovicum Elzebirium, 1652), pp. 10-11 and 13-14; Boëthius, De Musica, i, p. 10; E. Krenek, "Proportionen und pythagoräische Hämmer," Musica, 14 (1960), 708-712.

[3]F. Kuttner, Bericht über den siebenten internationalen musikwissenschaftlichen Kongress, Köln 1958, p. 174. It should be noted that this scale was known in China and was possibly used there before its use in Greece.

[4]Iamblichus, iii, p. 4.

[5]Iamblichus, Nikom. Arith. Intro. (Ed. by Pistelli), p. 10.

[6]Henry George Farmer, Historical Facts for the Arabian Musical Influence (London: William Reeves, n.d.), p. 126.

[7]Philo Judaeus, vi, pp. 32-33.

[8]Farmer, pp. 126-127.

[9]In discussing Greek music, it must be remembered that "harmony" and "harmonics" meant agreement as in tuning. Harmonic theory dealt with the division of musical space (a scale or mode), not our modern concept of chord movement. (See Plato, Laws 812d-e for a discussion of "polyphony.")

[10]W. K. C. Guthrie, A History of Greek Philosophy (Cambridge: Cambridge University Press, 1962), I, p. 206.

[11]Censorius, De Die Natali, p. xiii.

[12]G. M. A. Grube, Plato's Thought (Boston: Beacon Press, 1958), pp. 179-180, 187.

[13]Will Durant, The Life of Greece (New York: Simon and Schuster, 1939), pp. 451, 455.

[14]Władysław Tatarkiewicz, History of Aesthetics (Warszawa: PWN-Polish Scientific Publishers, 1970), I, p. 126.

[15]Plato, Gorgias 501e.   (Translations of Plato are those in Hamilton & Cairns, The Collected Dialogues of Plato.)

[16]E. Diehl, Anthologia Lyrica Graeca (Leipzig, 1942), II, 150, no. 7.

[17]Plato, Republic 397a-b.

[18]Isobel Henderson, "Ancient Greek Music," in New Oxford History of Music (London: Oxford University Press, 1957), I, p. 402.

[19]Aristotle, Metaphysics 985b-986a, 109a, 1093a-b, trans. W. D. Ross; De caelo 290b, trans. J. L. Stocks.

[20]There are two notable exceptions to this rigorous empiricism: 1) Politica 1254a (trans. Benjamin Jowett) illustrates the idea of a ruling principle even in inanimate things, e.g., the harmoniai.   The "ruling principle" in this passage has been interpreted as some metaphysical law permeating the universe.   One need not so interpret the passage.   The section concerns the distinction between rulers and subjects.   Aristotle says that such a distinction exists in all life and belongs to the very constitution of the universe.   "Even in things which have no life there is a ruling principle, as in musical mode."   Aristotle is probably thinking of the note mese, which is found in any harmonia, and functions like our tonic.   Tonic-mese rules the key-harmonia, all notes gravitate to it as "home."   There is nothing metaphysical in this statement, it merely describes the function of the mese in the modes; 2) <Plutarch> in his Peri mousikes 1139 § 23 says that Aristotle called the harmoniai celestial because their

nature is divine, noble and marvellously wrought, but
<Plutarch> does not give the source of his information.

[21]Aristotle, Politics 1339a.

[22]Ibid., 1339b.

[23]Ibid., 1341a.

[24]Ibid., 1341b.

[25]Ibid., 1338a.

[26]Most scholars agree that the Problemata are not
Aristotle's. He wrote a book of problems (listed in
Diogenes Laertius, Philosophers' Lives, V, 23) and some
of these may be from his hand. Nevertheless, it is
generally agreed the Problemata are a product of the
Peripatetic School. For a more detailed account of this
work see: W. S. Hett's introduction of his translation
(Cambridge: Harvard University Press, 1970); Karl von
Jan, Musici Scriptores Graeci (Lipsiae: Teubneri, 1895),
pp. 39-111; Alexis Kahl, Die Philosophie der Musik nach
Aristoteles (Leipzig: Breitkopf & Härtel, 1902).

[27]<Aristotle>, Problemata, XIX, paras. 1, 23. it
should be noted that the question in para. 23 is
identical to the question in Sense and the Sensible
447a 7.

[28]Aristoxenus, Harmonics, trans. and ed. by Henry
S. Macran (Oxford: Clarendon Press, 1902). This volume
has been reprinted by Georg Olms. Since all references
to Aristoxenus are from this work, the numbers written
thus <2> refer to the marginal numbers in Macran's Greek
and English text.

[29]For an edition, transcription and translation of
all extant examples of ancient Greek music both vocal
and instrumental see Egert Pöhlmann, Denkmäler
altgriechischer Musik: Sammlung, übertragung und
Erläuterung aller Fragmente und Fälschungen (Nürnberg:
Hans Carl, 1970). Examples of instrumental music are on
pp. 36-40, 98, 104.

[30]Plato, Laws 669d-e, 700a-701a.

[31]Paul Marquard, ed., Die harmonischen Fragmente
des Aristoxenus (Berlin: Wiedmannsche Buchhandlung,
1868).

[32]Ptolemy, Harmonikon, ed. by Ingemar Düring
(Göteborg: Elanders Boktryckeri Aktiebolag, 1930).

[33]Johannes Lohmann, Musiké und Logos (Stuttgart:
Musikwissenschaftliche Verlags-Gesellschaft m.b.H.,
1970), p. 58. "Dessen Bezeichnungs-System ist aber der
Geometrie, also einer streng wissenschaftlichen
Bezeichnung-Methode entlehnt und hat nichts mit der
Praxis zu tun." <my translation>

[34]Adler, pp. 16-17.

[35]Jan, pp. 179-207. There is a complete English
translation in W. O. Strunk, Source Readings in Music
History (New York: W. W. Norton, 1950), pp. 34-46.

[36]Athenaeus, The Deipnosophists, trans. C. B.
Gulick (Cambridge: Harvard University Press, 1937).

[37]Ibid., XIV, 633b-c.

[38]Plato, Philebus 56a. <underline mine>

[39]This quartet of studies goes all the way back to
the Sophists in Plato's day. Protagoras tells us that
"ordinary sophists" teach arithmetic, astronomy, geometry and music, whereas he will teach good judgment in
personal and civic affairs. See Plato, Protagoras 318e.

[40]Martin Gerbert, Scriptores Ecclesiastici de
Musica Sacra Potissimum (Hildesheim: Georg Olms, 1963),
I, p. 195.

[41]Regino of Prüm, De Harmonica Institutione, in
Jacques Paul Migne, Patrologiae Cursus Completus
(Latina) (Parisiis: J. P. Migne, 1844-1864), CXXXII,
p. 494.

[42]Gerbert, I, p. 172. One cannot help think of
Aristotle's Politics 1254s. <see fn. 27>

[43]John Scotus Eriugena, De Divisione Naturae, in
Migne, CXXII, p. 965.

[44]Dominicus Gundissalinus in Martin Grabmann,
Geschichte der scholastischen Methode (Freiberg in
Breisgau, 1909), II, p. 100.

[45]Regino of Prüm, De Harm. Inst., 18.

[46]John Cotton, Musica, in Gerbert, II, p. 233.

[47]Augustine, De Musica, in Migne, XXXII, pp. 1081-
1194. English translation in The Fathers of the Church,
ed. R. J. Deferrari; trans. R. C. Taliaferro (New York:
Fathers of the Church, Inc., 1947), IV, pp. 153-379.

[48]Augustine, De Musica, IV, 6, 16.

[49]Ibid., VI, 2, 2-5.

[50]Ibid., VI, 12, 35.

[51]Ibid., VI, 1, 1.

[52]Ibid., I, 2, 2.

[53]Martianus Capella, De Nuptiis Philologiae et
Mercurii, ed. A. Dick (Leipzig: Teubner, 1925). See
also Meibom, II, pp. 165-198 (text); pp. 339-363
(notes). There is an English translation in Martianus
Capella and the Seven Liberal Arts, ed. & trans. W. H.
Stahl, et al. (New York: Columbia University Press,
1977). References are to section numbers which
correspond in the Dick and Stahl editions. Note that
Gustave Reese, in his Music in the Middle Ages (New
York: W. W. Norton & Co., 1940), p. 125, no. 7, refers
to the De Nuptiis as the Satyricon.

[54]Boëthius, De Institutione Arithmetica, libri duo.
De Institutione Musica, libri quinque, ed. G. Friedlein
(Lipsiae, 1867). All references are to this edition.
An English translation has been done by Calvin M. Bower,

"Boëthius' The Principles of Music, an Introduction, Translation, and Commentary," Diss. George Peabody College of Teachers, 1966.

[55]Cassiodorus, Variae, in Migne, LXIX, p. 589.

[56]For a thorough analysis of Boëthius' sources see Bower, pp. 333-369.

[57]Boëthius, De Inst. Mus., I, 34.

[58]Ibid., I, 10.

[59]Ibid., IV, 1.

[60]Boëthius, Topicorum Aristotelis Interpretatio, III, 1, in Migne, LXIV, p. 935.

[61]Boëthius, De Inst. Mus., I, 34.

[62]Bower, p. 23.

[63]Ibid., pp. 457-460.

[64]Cassiodorus, De Artibus ac Disciplinis Liberalium Litterarum. De Musica, in Migne, LXX, pp. 1203-1212. All references are to this edition. An English version is in W. O. Strunk, Source Readings in Music History (New York: W. W. Norton, 1950), pp. 87-92.

[65]Cassiodorus, De Musica, pp. 1203-1204.

[66]Ibid., p. 1209.

[67]Ibid.

[68]Meibom, pp. 11-13.

[69]Isidore of Seville, Etymologiarum sive Originum, libri XX. De Musica, ed. W. M. Lindsay (Oxonii: Clarendoniano, 1911), I, lib. III, xv-xxiii. All references are to this edition. An English translation is in Strunk, pp. 93-100.

[70]Isidore of Seville, De Musica, III, 15.

[71]Isidore writes: "_Sambuca_ _in_ _musicis_ _species_ _est_
symphoniarum." Strunk (p. 97) translates _symphonia_
as"drum," which, in this context, is too specific.
Isidore seems to be using the word generically to mean
"musical instrument." A better translation might be:
"The sambuca, among musicians, is a kind of musical
instrument." Isidore writes _in_ _musicis_ because the
sambuca was also an instrument of warfare. At the end
of § 22 Isidore does describe a drum as _symphonia_,
but with the qualification that this use is the _vulgo_
appellatur.

[72]Boëthius, _De_ _Inst_. _Mus_., II, 17.

[73]What does all this mean? Arithmetic mean a of
two numbers m and n is determined: $m-a=a-n$ and the
harmonic mean h by the relationship: $1/m-1/h=1/h-1/n$.
Thus $a=1/2(m+n)$, and $h=2mn/m+n$. Boëthius demonstrated
that the arithmetic mean of the octave is a fifth and
the harmonic mean is the fourth. In other words, it is
a mathematical demonstration, so dear to these writers,
of the P4th and P5th.

[74]Isidore of Seville, _De_ _Ecclesiasticis_ _Officiis_,
in Migne, LXXIII, p. 743.

[75]Odo of Cluny, _Dialogus_ _de_ _Musica_, in Gerbert, I,
pp. 251-264. The tonary is also in Gerbert, I, pp. 248-
250. For a thorough study of the many tonaries
attributed to Odo see: Michel Huglo, _Les_ _Tonaires_
(Paris: Société Française de Musicologie, 1971),
pp. 182-224, 325.

[76]Gerbert, I, p. 256.

[77]Joannes, monk of Cluny, _St_. _Odo_ _of_ _Cluny_, trans.
Dom Gerard Sitwell (London: Sheed and Ward, 1958),
pp. 3-87.

[78]Ibid., p. xxvi.

[79]Ex MS. biblioth. reg. Paris. 7211.

[80]Strunk, _Source_ _Readings_, p. 103. Gerbert, I,
p. 251.

[81]Ibid., p. 104. Gerbert, I, p. 251.

[82]Ibid., p. 109. Gerbert, I, p. 255.

[83]Ibid., p. 113. Gerbert, I, p. 257.

[84]Gerbert, I, pp. 248-250.

[85]Ibid., p. 249.

[86]Huglo, Les Tonaires, p. 207.

[87]Hugo Riemann, History of Music Theory, trans. Raymond H. Haggh (Lincoln: University of Nebraska Press, 1962), p. 352, fn. 4.

[88]Henry George Farmer, "The Music of Islam," in New Oxford History of Music (London: Oxford University Press, 1957), I, pp. 468-469.

[89]Farmer, Historical Facts of the Arabian Musical Influence, pp. 31, 94.

[90]Guido d'Arezzo, Regulae musicae de ignoto cantu, in Gerbert, II, p. 35. An English translation is in Strunk, Source Readings, pp. 117-120. See also Guidonis "Prologus in Antiphonarium," ed. J. Smits van Waesberghe (Frits Knuf, 1975), p. 62.

[91]Guido d'Arezzo, Micrologus in Gerbert, II, pp. 2-24. There are two English versions: Albin Dunstan McDermott, "The 'Micrologus' of Guido d'Arezzo," Master's thesis. University of Pittsburgh, 1929 and W. Babb in Hucbald, Guido, and John on Music: Three Medieval Treatises, ed. C. V. Palisca (New Haven: Yale University Press, 1979). A critical edition was done by Jos. Smits van Wesberghe, Guidonis Aretini Micrologus (s.l.: American Institute of Musicology, 1955). All references in this work will be to chapters, e.g., Micrologus, 13.

[92]In Gerbert, II, 25-33.

[93]Guido d'Arezzo, Epistola de ignoto cantu, in Gerbert, II, p. 43-50. There is an English translation

in Strunk, Source Readings, pp. 121-125, however, this translation is not complete omitting Gerbert, II, 46a/10 to 50b/11.

[94]Micrologus, 5.

[95]Ibid.

[96]Ibid., 2.

[97]Ibid., 17.

[98]Władysław Tatarkiewicz, History of Aesthetics (Warszawa: PWN-Polish Scientific Publishers, 1970), II, p. 129.

[99]Strunk, Source Readings, p. 124.

[100]Micrologus, 20.

[101]Cassiodorus, Institutiones, 9. See also Strunk, Source Readings, pp. 91-92.

[102]This work is the first thirteen chapters of Philippe de Vitry's Ars Nova, eds., Gilbert Reany et al. (s.l.: American Institute of Musicology, 1964). There is an English translation by Leon Plantinga in the Journal of Music Theory, V (1961), pp. 204-223. All references to this work are by chapter number.

[103]Erich Reimer, Johannes de Garlandia: De Mensurabili Musica (Wiesbaden: Franz Steiner, 1972). There is an English translation by Stanley H. Birnbaum, Concerning Measured Music (Colorado Springs: Colorado College Music Press, 1978). All references to this work are by chapter number.

[104]William G. Waite, "Johannes de Garlandia, poet and musician," Speculum, 35 (1960), pp. 179-195.

[105]Rome, Bib. Vaticana lat.5325; Paris, Bib. Nationale lat.18514; Rome, Bib. Vaticana Barberini lat.307 (P. de Vitry's Ars Nova, chapters 1-13).

[106]De Musica Plana, 1.

[107]Ibid., 2.

[108]It is interesting to note that this same liquid etymology is given in John Cotton's De Musica Cum Tonario (Waesberghe, 1950), p. 55: "Alii musicam quasi modusicam a modulatione, alii quasi moysicam ab aqua, quae moys dicitur, appellatam optimantur." A comment is in order: the moys must be a form of musa or the muses; ycos could be icos which is Greek eikos which means reasonable and is close enough to knowledge. Thus we get mus + ic(a). How the water managed to seep in is beyond me. One might speculate on the tradition that the muses of music, Euterpe or Calliope, were the mothers of the Thracian King Rhesus, his father being the river god Strymon.

[109]De Mensurabili Musica, 1.

[110]Ibid., 7.

[111]Ibid., 2.

[112]Ibid., 2, 3. Also De Plana Musica, 9. What this means is that now it is possible to notate durational changes in either the beginning (propriety) or the ending (perfection) of a ligature. A ligature is a notational device that combines two or more notes in a single symbol.

[113]Ibid., 9.

[114]Ibid.

[115]Ibid.

[116]Johannes de Garlandia, Concerning Measured Music, trans. Stanley H. Birnbaum (Colorado Springs: Colorado College Music Press, 1978), p. 58.

[117]Franco of Cologne, Ars Cantus Mensurabilis, ed. Gilbert Reany and A. Gilles (s.l.: American Institute of Musicology, 1974). There is an English translation in Strunk, Source Readings, pp. 139-159. All references to this work are by chapter number.

[118]Ars Cantus Mensurabilis, Prologue.

[119]Ibid., 3.

[120]Ibid., 4, 5.

[121]Ibid., 9.

[122]Gustave Reese, Music in the Middle Ages (New York: W. W. Norton & Company, 1940), p. 289.

[123]See fn. 109. All references to this work are by chapter number.

[124]Ernest H. Sanders, "Vitry, Philippe de," New Grove Dictionary of Music and Musicians, 1980 ed.

[125]Philippe de Vitry, Ars Nova, 15-18.

[126]Ibid., 9.

[127]Willi Apel, Harvard Dictionary of Music, p. 427. Some major sources for these isorhythmic motets are the Chantilly MSS., Muse Condé 1047; Modena MSS., Biblioteca Estanse L. 568; Roman de Fauvel, Paris, Bib. nationale fonds frc. 146; Codex Ivrea (Italy); and Guillaume de Machaut, The Works of Guillaume de Machaut, ed. Leo Schrade. Monaco: Editions de l'oiseau-lyre, 1956.

[128]Pope John's Bull is in the Oxford History of Music (1929) in Latin and English, pp. 294-296.

[129]Musica Enchiriadis is in Martin Gerbert, Scriptores ecclesiastici de musica, I, pp. 152-173.

[130]Tatarkiewicz, History of Aesthetics, II, p. 129.

[131]See fn. 50.

[132]Johannes Tinctoris, Dictionary of Musical Terms (Terminorum Musicae Diffinitorium), trans. Carl Parrish (London: Collier Macmillan, Ltd., 1963). Text in English and Latin from the incunabulum in the British Museum.

[133]Karl Weinmann, Johannes Tinctoris und sein
unbekannter Traktat "De inventione et usu musicae"
(Tutzing: Hans Schneider, 1961).

[134]Johannes Tinctoris, The Art of Counterpoint
(Liber de Arte Contrapuncti), trans. Albert Seay (s.l.:
American Institute of Musicology, 1961).

[135]Tinctoris, Terminorum Musicae Diffinitorium,
p. 3 (underline mine).

[136]Ibid., 43.

[137]Ibid., 45.

[138]What has come down to us are two chapters each of
Books II, III, IV that Tinctoris sent to Johannes
Stokhem.

[139]Weinmann, Johannes Tinctoris, p. 33.

[140]Ibid., pp. 34-46.

[141]Johannes Tinctoris, The Art of Counterpoint,
p. 14.

[142]Ibid., p. 14.

[143]Ibid., pp. 102-105.

[144]Ibid., p. 132.

[145]Tinctoris, Terminorum Musicae Diffinitorium,
p. 25.

[146]Tinctoris, Complexus effectum musices, in
Coussemaker, IV, p. 192.

[147]Tinctoris, Terminorum Musicae Diffinitorium,
p. 15.

[148]Pietro Aron, Libri Tres de Institutione
Harmonica (Bologna: Forni, 1970).   This is a facsimile
of Coll.B.8 in the Civico Museo Bibliografico Musicale
di Bologna.

[149]Ibid., Bk. III, chaps. 7-9.

[150]Pietro Aron, Toscanello in Music, trans. Peter Bergquist (Colorado Springs: Colorado College Music Press, 1970).

[151]Ibid., Bk. II, suppl. p. 20.

[152]Ibid., Bk. II, chap. 41, p. 10. This tuning has pure thirds and fifths flattened by 1/4 of a comma.

[153]Heinrich Glarean, Isagoge in Musicen, trans. Frances Berry Turrell, Journal of Music Theory, 3 (1959), pp. 97-139.

[154]Heinrich Glarean, Dodecachordon, trans. Clement A. Miller (s.l.: American Institute of Musicology, 1965).

[155]Heinrich Glarean, Musicae Epitome Sive Compendium ex Glareani Dodecachordo (Basel: Heinrich Petri, 1557).

[156]Glarean, Isagoge, pp. 129-130.

[157]Glarean, Dodecachordon, p. 150.

[158]Ibid., p. 250.

[159]Ibid., p. 38.

[160]Ibid., p. 41.

[161]Gioseffo Zarlino, Le Istitutioni Harmoniche (Venice: Francesco Senese, 1562). There are the following translations and commentaries: Book III: The Art of Counterpoint, trans. Guy A. Marco and Claude V. Palisca (New Haven: Yale University Press, 1968); Book IV: "Zarlino on Modes," trans. Cohen Vered, Diss. City University of New York, 1967; Books III and IV: Strunk, Source Readings, pp. 229-261 (these are selections).

[162]Gioseffo Zarlino, Sopplimento Musicali (Venice, 1588; rpt. Ridgewood: Gregg Press, 1966).

[163]Gioseffo Zarlino, Dimonstrati Harmoniche
(Venice, 1571; rpt. Farnborough: Gregg Press, 1966).

[164]Zarlino, Istitutioni Harmoniche, iv, 33.

[165]Zarlino, The Art of Counterpoint, p. 1.

[166]Zarlino, Istitutioni Harmoniche, i. 2.

[167]Ibid., iv, 36. Vered, p. 237.

[168]Zarlino, Istitutioni Harmoniche, i, 3.

[169]Nicola Vicentino, L'Antica Musica Ridotta alla
Moderna Prattica (Rome: 1555; rpt. Kassel:
Bärenreiter, 1959).

[170]Ibid., fol. 16.

[171]Galileo Galilei, Two New Sciences, trans.
Stillman Drake (Madison: The University of Wisconsin
Press, 1974).

CHAPTER III

A RETROSPECTIVE OF MUSICOLOGY (PART II)

§ 6. The Age of Reason

Where the Renaissance gave European man his
individuality, the Enlightenment brought to fruition his
rational powers. The process of fruition was aided by
the work of two men who wrote at the crossroads of the
Renaissance and the Age of Reason. Indeed, one might
conjecture that the temper of the Age of Reason is due
to their work in the natural sciences, mathematics and
philosophy. Galileo Galilei, through practical
application and the use of mathematics, demonstrated the
usability of scientific methods long dormant in the
European mind. René Descartes gave philosophical
grounding to these scientific methods by showing that
there is an objective world, that can be studied and
mathematized, separate from the mind of the mathe-
matizer.[1] The world is now a "dueverse" of the
irreducible parts res cogitans and res extensa,[2] and
this world has now become measurable through a kind of
cosmic apodictic geometry. The res extensa of Descartes
is a mathematical manifold to mathematical idea. Reason
is declared the supreme tool for the ultimate
description and explanation of the universe. In the
Meditations, Descartes has provided "a radical

foundation for the new rationalism and then <u>eo</u> <u>ipso</u> for dualism."[3]

Music, being part of the <u>res extensa</u>, was a prime target for this mathematizing process. We have already seen how Galileo treated the subject in his dialogue. He was also well aware of the mathematization of music at the hands of the Pythagoreans and that music was considered to be one of the mathematical sciences. Two years before Galileo published his dialogue on science a Frenchman, Marin Mersenne (1588-1646), published his <u>Harmonie</u> <u>Universelle</u> (1636)[4] in which he was concerned, among many other things, with string vibrations and a mathematical way of discerning pitch. Independently of each other they came to the same conclusion about the relationship of string length, its tension and the resulting pitch.[5] What this method amounts to is a scientific-mathematical way of determining the pitch of a string without ever hearing it. Acoustics has come of age.

Two other branches of the growing science of music receive elaboration from Mersenne: pedagogy and organology.   His pedagogical inquires concern the teaching of music to children and beginners.[6] In the area of organology he describes the structure and abilities of both Western and Eastern musical instruments.[7]

René Descartes' <u>Compendium</u> <u>Musicae</u> (1618; pub. 1650) is another work which had a great influence on subsequent writers in the Age of Reason.[8] The most direct influence was on Descartes' friend and

correspondent Marin Mersenne. Many letters passed
between the two dealing with musical matters and some of
this material found its way into Mersenne's Harmonie
Universelle and his Questiones harmoniques, de la Nature
des Sons (1635).

For our project, Descartes' work is important in
several ways, but the most important is his use of an
empirical, scientific method to study auditory
phenomena. Descartes' musical theories and methods were
to have a direct influence on Joseph Sauveur through the
lectures of the Cartesian physicist Jacques Rohault.
J.-P. Rameau, later on, was to use Descartes' method in
his harmonic studies. Among Descartes' contributions is
his theory of the harmonic series and sympathetic vibration[9]; his constant use of mathematics to describe the
heard, not just a theoretical "heard"; and his attempt
to correlate, in a scientific manner, the physical and
psychological (emotional) aspects of music. He draws
our attention to our emotional consciousness of duration
and the musical use of divisions of duration, e.g., "I
will say that in general a slower pace arouses in us
quieter feelings such as langour, sadness . . . a faster
pace arouses faster emotions, such as joy, etc."[10]

In general, Descartes' approach to music is
threefold: scientific-objective, practical, and
subjective. The scientific part of this triad is his
mathematization of musical sound and discussions of its
physical attributes, i.e., acoustics. The practical
part delves into the nature of sensory perception. As
he states at the beginning of the work, "the noise of
guns or thunder is not fit for music, because it

injures the ear."[11] The subjective aspect deals with
the effects of perception on the listener. These musings
are not scientific in nature and are part of an aesthetics or metaphysics of music. They stem, in part,
from the Platonic corpus and will be picked up later on
by German theorists, most notably Mattheson, and turned
into the Doctrine of the Affections.

a.   Joseph Sauveur, 1653-1716

Sauveur's contribution to musical knowledge can be
summed up in one word: acoustics. He disseminated his
musical ideas through the publications of the Royal
Academy of Sciences (1701-1713).[12] His works include:
"General System of Intervals," "Application of Harmonics
to the Composition of Organ Stops," "General Method of
Forming the Tempered Systems of Music...," "General
Table of the Tempered Systems of Music," and "Relationship of the Sounds of Strings of Musical Instruments..."

Sauveur's work on the phenomenon of music can be
divided into four major ideas: duration, division of
the octave into 3,010 equal parts, pitch determination
through frequency, and the harmonic series arising from
the vibration of a string.

For the measurement of duration, Sauveur used a
chronometer, which he defines as "a rule consisting of
several divided lines which serve as scales for
measuring the duration of sounds and for finding their
intervals and ratios."[13] The duration was measured
by Sauveur's pendulum device.[14]

In the paper, "General System...," Sauveur proceeds
to describe his division of the octave, this coming
after a discussion of the problems inherent in the
various tuning systems that music has used.[15] "The
octave is divided into 43 equal parts, which he calls
'meridians', and the division of each meridian into seven
equal intervals, which he calls 'heptameridians'." For
Sauveur these do not indicate the intervals as accurately as he felt could be so he divides the heptameridians into ten equal decameridians, thus the octave
is divided, finally, into 3,010 parts.[16] We have here
an extremely accurate measure for the fluctuation of
vibration between intervals in various tuning systems.

In § I of the "General System...", Sauveur
describes how one can compare two pitches "by the ratio
of the number of vibrations of one to the number of
vibrations of the other."[17] From this it can be determined what the interval is if the frequency of the
vibration is known. Sauveur, as a reference point,
suggests: "take as fundamental the fixed sound, which
makes a hundred vibrations per second."[18]

Finally, he posits the harmonic series in § IX of
the same work.[19] The definition of harmonics that he
gives is quite simple: "I call a 'harmonic' of the
fundamental that which makes several vibrations while
the fundamental makes only one." He then proceeds to
give us the harmonics of five octaves. Through dividing
the string of the monochord, he gives us a method by
which we can make audible and divisible harmonics.[20]
This discovery and its scientific description revo-
lutionized the study of music. The acoustical or

physical properties of sound were substituted for purely
mathematical and speculative rationalizations. Physical
law, not pure mathematics, became the locus of questions
and answers in subsequent music theory.

Sauveur's work in acoustics is consciously
scientific and completely separated from music as music.
He compares his acoustics to the science of optics as
distinct from things seen:

> I have thus believed that there is a science
> superior to music, which I have called
> "Acoustics," which has as its object sound in
> general, whereas music has as its object
> sound in so far as it is agreeable to
> hearing.[21]

Sauveur was merely following the scientific ambition of
his age: an inventory and explanation of phenomena by
means of observation, experimentation and mathematical
analysis. He succeeded in spite of the natural obstacle
of having been born deaf.[22]

b.   Johann Fux, 1660-1741

As a composer, Fux contributed more than 500 works
to the musical output of his time. There are about 20
operas, 14 large sacred oratorios, 80 masses and many
instrumental pieces.[23]

As a theorist, Fux contributed one work: a book on
counterpoint, the Gradus ad Parnassum.[24] This

counterpoint book, as Blume writes, "lent canonic
validity" to late Renaissance (stile antico) music and
passed it on to subsequent centuries.[25] The Gradus of
Fux is considered the first modern textbook of counterpoint and is still used today as a beginning text for
teaching modal counterpoint.

The work is set as a dialogue between a student
named Josephus and the master Aloysius who is
Palestrina. Josephus has come to the master, Aloysius,
to learn the art of composition. Fux writes that his
reason for writing such a dialogue is "to help young
persons who want to learn." He especially wants to help
those who do not have the means nor a teacher. His
method is "similar to that by which children learn first
letters, then syllables, then combinations of syllables,
and finally how to read and write." Fux also wants us
to notice that this is a book of musical practice and he
has "given very little space to theory ... since (action
being the test of excellence) this was the greater
need."[26] The master takes the student through a course
in strict composition in the "Palestrina" style with
species counterpoint and ending with florid counterpoint
in four voices. The work concludes with a section on
free composition.

The importance of Fux's counterpoint cannot be
overestimated. Nearly all subsequent modal counterpoint
books have been modeled on or taken outright from Fux.
The list of composers who either studied or used Fux as
a text includes J. S. Bach, Beethoven, Haydn, Mozart,
Berlioz, Chopin, Liszt, etc. Such 20th-century writers

on counterpoint as Knud Jeppeson, Paul Hindemith and
Arnold Schoenberg all look back to Fux as their model.

c. Johann Mattheson, 1681-1764

Mattheson is one of those writers that defy
summation due to the encyclopedic nature of their work.
The best approach is to consider, one at a time, each of
his major works on music, their main points, and then
attempt a textual and methodological summary of his
contributions to musicology.

Das neu-eröffnete Orchestre (1713) is his first
critical work.[27] This work is in three sections:
musical terminology, rules and principles of compositions, and analytical criticism. Section one is a compendium of those musical terms and concepts that every
educated music listener should know. Section two, on
composition, takes the reader through the general rules
of counterpoint and the differences between consonance
and dissonance. The last chapter of this section is on
the different kinds of compositions, e.g., church music,
opera and chamber music and the forms that pertain to
each. The last section is on analytical criticism
(judicatoria). Mattheson opens this section with
stylistic descriptions of Italian, French, English and
German music. Chapter two is an exposition of the loci
topici so loved by the 18th century. These writers,
taking their cue from the ancients, believed that music
could have an emotional effect on the listener and that
these affects could be codified in "figures," the loci
topici which would represent the affection in music.

There was thought to be an analogy between rhetorical figures and musical figures as in the recitative: music and words are inextricably bound together. Mattheson points out the general characteristics of the various keys and the emotional qualities of each, e.g., E-minor is thoughtful and sad. Writing in this key should convey such sadness to the listener.[28] The work ends with a supplement devoted to the question: which is deemed higher, music or painting?[29] In the course of this discussion Mattheson hits upon one of the major debates of his time, that between the rationalists and the empiricists on the ground of music. Is it mathematics or nature? Mattheson seems to lean to the empirical side when he writes: "where has the little bird learned singing and twittering, it hasn't been to the Pythagorean school..."[30] He goes on to claim that the origins of music are first in God and then in Nature.[31]

Das forschende Orchestre (1721) is basically a defense of the senses as participating in the artistic process.[32] He also expands the rational basis for the loci topici found in the previous work. As Harriss has written, Mattheson sees himself as the Aristoxenus the Younger fighting against a Pythagorean antagonist: let the ear be the judge not mathematics in the question of dissonance-consonance.[33]

The Criteria Musica (1722-1725), edited and written in part by Mattheson, is important as the first German music periodical devoted to informative music criticism. The issues contain letters, translations, articles and news items all written in an approachable popular style.

Mattheson's major work is his Der Vollkommene
Capellmeister (1739).[34]   Here is Mattheson's musical
compendium. As Harriss writes of it:

In this large volume, he endeavored to impart
in detail all the practical, theoretical,
historical, and philosophical wisdom which had
concerned him for many years.[35]

The work is meant as a guide for the competent chapel
master of the 18th century, and contains all the tools
of his trade.

The work is divided into three large sections:
Part I deals with those elements of musical erudition
that are considered basic; Part II is on the essence of
melodic science, i.e., music's foundation; and Part III
is an exposition of those principles inherent in more
complex compositional problems. This last part, also,
contains a section on organology: organ building (one
of the more important to come out of the Baroque).
Chapter 25 of this section, "The Art of Playing", is
important for performance practices of the 18th century,
in so far as he discusses orchestration problems, styles
of organ-playing appropriate for various occasions,
improvisation, etc. He concludes with a chapter on
conducting, producing and directing a concert.

Also, Mattheson continues his musings on the loci
topici.[36]   These are in the character of elaborations
of the previous discussion.

Methodologically, Mattheson seems to be a synthesis of Descartes' rationalism and Locke's empiricism. Descartes' method, as used by Mattheson, can be summarized in these steps: avoid bias (clear recognition), divide up a problem, engage the question a step at a time, and be thorough. Mattheson uses this method in his analysis of melody-writing.[37] First, he shows how melody is clearly the generator of all music, and presents the reader with the opposing view that harmony is the essence of music.[38] Second, he demonstrates how difficult it is to teach melody-writing without a "thorough differentiation and explanation" of harmony and melody before a "proper classification" can be undertaken.[39] Third, the data gleaned in the classification are reflected upon in due order: significance of intervals, generation of monophony, growth of harmony, etc.[40] Lastly, Mattheson follows with pages of examples to underscore his method "of making a good melody." One other aspect of a good melody that bears a comparison with Descartes is that a melody must not only be simple, but clear and distinct.[41] Descartes demanded the same of any idea before it be accepted apodictically. Clarity and distinctness of idea is required before the analysis of a problem. For Mattheson, a clear and distinct melody is the prerequisite for a good piece of music; after all, the essence of music is melody.[42]

The Lockean aspect of Mattheson is that practical experience is the ideal teacher--not just the use of Reason. As Mattheson writes: "Science differs from art in that it comprehends a matter through reasoning only, whereas art requires practical application as an

inseparable component."[43] First comes experience,
without which we are musical tabulae rasae, then comes
Reason to explain the experience.

Mattheson's excursion into music dictionaries is
his Grundlage einer Ehrenpforte (1740).[44] This work
contains the biographies of 148 prominent musicians of
his day. One notable exception is that of J. S. Bach.
He seems not to have returned Mattheson's questionnaire!

Finally, Mattheson wrote three works on thorough-
bass: Exemplarische Organtisten-Probe (1719)[45] and the
Kleine and Grosse General-Bass-Schule (1735, 1731).[46]
In addition to writing these as handbooks on thorough-
bass, Mattheson advocates equal temperament, gives practical examples in all keys, and has one of the first
discussions on the use of double sharps and flats and
the natural sign.[47] With the final triumph of the
tonal system and the spread of equal temperament, the
use of these accidentals was problematic.

Mattheson not only wrote compendia on all aspects
of music (for this alone he is important for future
generations); he was also the founder of musical criticism, practical music theory (not speculative) and music
history in Germany.[48] As we shall see, the rise of
musicology as we know it owes much to Mattheson. He was
the ultimate musical rationalist in the Age of Reason.
Mattheson believed in the progress of music to better
and better productions and he codified and systematized
all aspects of music.

d.   Jean-Philippe Rameau, 1683-1764

Rameau is the first major theorist-musicologist
whose musical reputation is based as much upon his
compositions as on his theoretical writings. We must
concern ourselves principally with his theoretical
writings, and consider his compositional technique only
in so far as it bears on his theories.

Although Rameau penned some 33 items on music and
music theory, by far the most influential was his Traité
de l'harmonie (1722).[49] The title page tells us his
method, i.e., the reduction of harmony to its natural
principles, that it is conceived of as a scientific
treatise, and tells us its scope, i.e., the work will
cover harmonic ratios and proportions, the nature and
properties of chords, composition and the art of accompaniment.

In the preface Rameau shows himself to be a child
of the Age of Reason. Practicality and experience can
teach us a great deal about music; however, it is Reason
alone that can discover the principles behind the music
we experience. For Rameau, Reason must justify the
practices of music.[50] As so many before him, Rameau
sees music as a science

> which should have definite rules; these rules
> should be drawn from an evident principle;
> and this principle cannot be really known to
> us without the aid of mathematics.

Later on, Rameau tells us his purpose: "One must
conceptualize these efforts <of a science or an art> in
order to render them intelligible. That is the end to
which I have principally applied myself in the body of
this work...."[51]

The Traité is Rameau's attempt to ground the
principles of music in mathematics. Later on he became
aware of the work of Mersenne and Sauveur and he
"revised" his approach based on acoustics. The
resultant work is the Demonstration du Principe de
l'harmonie (1750).[52] Mathematics and the acoustical
properties of sonorous bodies are now combined. "These
proportions <harmonic, arithmetic and geometric> are
manifested in the first moment in which the sonorous
body resonates...."[53] This union of mathematics and
acoustics was to serve "as the basis for the complete
art of theoretical and practical music."[54] Later on in
his life Rameau attempted a universalization of his
musical principles into a cosmology by showing that
music stems from some natural cosmic principle of
unity.[55]

Out of the mass of theoretical writings, the major
contribution of Rameau to musicology is the concept of
functional harmony.[56] Rameau came to this concept
through an understanding of the harmonic implications of
tonal centers (keys). Glarean noticed the same implications in the "hidden relationships of the modes." Two
centuries later Rameau is scientifically describing this
relationship. As he states in the Traité,

> we have designated that note by which the
> bass begins and ends as the tonic note, and
> we have said that it determines the
> progression of the other notes included
> within its octave.[57]

Harmonic tension-release and progression is determined
by the force of the tonic note. Coupled with this
progression of notes-chords, Rameau discovered the concept of chord inversions and that chords were built up
in thirds. Using Descartes' Method as a point of
enlightenment, Rameau noticed that an octave is a repli-
cate of itself: an E is an E no matter what range it is
in. He could invert an octave and it would remain the
same interval. As he states:

> The octave multiplies intervals, because when
> one believes he is hearing only a third, like
> ut to mi, he also hears a sixth between the
> same mi and the octave above this ut. In thus
> multiplying intervals, the octave indicates
> the possible inversion of intervals.[58]

He also noticed that the harmonic series is built up in
octaves, fifths and thirds, and that all chords can be
built up following the natural series. He went on to
note that all melody and harmony can be reduced to and
function in relation to the three mentioned chords (I,
V, IV).[59] From all of this comes the concept of
functional harmony, and the major-minor tonal system, in
use for such a long time, was given its theoretical and
systematic grounding.

Rameau also paid close attention to the use of the
loci topici in his theoretical writings and in his
music. In the Traité he notes that "harmony may
unquestionably excite different passions in us depending
on the chords that are used."[60] He goes on to give
examples of various passions and how to stimulate them
musically. Cheerful and pompous music demands consonant
chords; sweetness by "well prepared minor dissonances";
despair by all manner of unprepared dissonances.[61] He
is not as exact when it comes to the rhetorical use of
melody but finds it no less expressive than harmony.
Music is almost the text's servant and the rhetoric of
the text dictates the music.

> A good musician should surrender himself to
> all the characters he wishes to portray.
> Like a skillful actor he should take the
> place of the speaker....He must declaim the
> text well....[62]

Rameau's accentuation of the rôle of chords
(harmony) in music over that of melody shows him to be
in the musical avant-garde of his day. Melody was
always of secondary importance for Rameau. The contrapuntal music of the Baroque was passé and, as Bukofzer
writes, "Rameau's system of functional harmony represents the beginning of a new era of harmonic thought
<and> forms the transition to the theory of the classi-
cal period."[63]

e. Jean-Jacques Rousseau, 1712-1778

This Swiss musician and philosopher contributed,
through musical compositions and writings about music,
a wealth of material. Holding to our project, we will
restrict ourselves to a consideration of his contributions to musicology. Three such areas emerge from a
study of Rousseau's musical writing: theory, i.e., a
notation system; lexicography; and aesthetics.

His system of notation was first presented to the
Royal Academy of Science in a paper called "Projet
concernant de nouveaux Signes de musique" (1742), and
later published as "Dissertation sur la Musique moderne"
(1743).[64] Rousseau opens the "Projet" with a statement
of purpose:

> This project tends to render music more
> convenient to notate, easier to learn, and
> much less prolix.[65]

This notation is much more economical than "old style"
notation since it will be easier to print as it uses no
staves. His aesthetic attitudes are also operative in
this notation system as it is best suited to vocal music
and not instrumental. More on this point later.

A few notational concepts and devices will suffice
to show how it works. The pitches of the scale (C-B)
are replaced by the numbers (ciphers) 1 through 7.

Ex. 6.   Rousseauian Cipher Notation

To notate an octave change, a dot is placed over the
cipher for an octave higher.   For an octave lower, a dot
is placed under the cipher.[66]   Accidentals are notated
with a line through the cipher, e.g., 5, or G becomes 5̷,
or G♯.[67]   The following example shows how Rousseau
tackled the problem of notating duration.

Ex. 7.   Rousseauian Duration Notation

The lines above the 2 and 3 mean that those two notes
have the same combined durational value as the preceding
note, the 1.   The comma denotes that all three notes
(1 2̄ 3) have the same combined durational value as the 4
alone.   Rests are notated as 0.[68]   Two things militated
against this system being adopted on a general scale.

First, the monumental force of tradition was against it,
and second, it was conceived for vocal music and not the
large instrumental-orchestral pieces that were laying
hold of the musical imagination at this time. It is
technically impractical to write a symphonic score in
this cipher notation.

In the rarefied air of lexicography, Rousseau was
much more successful. He started his dictionary of
music in 1755, finished it in 1765 and published it in
1767.[69] His purpose is stated in the preface to the
work:

> Music is, of all the fine arts, the one which
> the vocabulary is most heard <u>entendu</u> and
> for which a dictionary is, consequently, most
> useful.[70]

He goes on to tell us that there have been many inferior
music dictionaries published and that he hopes his will
clear the air. The dictionary is an outgrowth of the
articles he wrote for Diderot's Encyclopédie (1751).
The dictionary contains no biographical sketches or
material; it is just a subject-dictionary. It is unique
in that there are entries for oriental music. Also,
there is, in the supplement of examples, a Chinese
melody that was later used by Weber and Hindemith as the
theme for musical compositions. An entry will suffice
to show the mood of the articles:

> BAROQUE. A baroque music is one in which the
> whole harmony is confused, filled with
> modulations and dissonances, the song hard

and unnatural, the intonation difficult, and
the movement constrained. It seems evident
that this term comes from the baroco of the
logicians.[71]

There are many rather subjective entries, covering the
gamut of music history and music theory. The work is
important because it set the tone and style for subsequent music dictionaries.

At the bottom of Rousseau's aesthetic beliefs was a
fundamental faith in the ancient Greek ideals of clarity
and simplicity. Apollonian musical style and the
inseparability of music and text were his watchwords.
Concomitant to this Apollonian attitude was his belief
that melody is the natural basis for music, not harmony as
with Rameau. In his dictionary he says that "natural" can
have several meanings: produced by the human voice
whereas artificial music is produced by instruments;
melodies are natural that are easy, sweet and pleasing;
"harmony is natural when it has few variations or
dissonances, when it is produced by chords essential to
the mode"; and finally, that music is natural which is
neither forced nor obscure.[72] Rousseau's music follows
these aesthetic tenets to the letter.

It is no wonder that he entered the lists in the
War of the Buffons on the side of melody and simplicity.
This war was the genesis of his opera Le Devin du
village, his French answer to the Italian opera buffa.
What he created was opéra comique. Hard on the heels of
this opera is his "Lettre sur la musique françoise," which
contains his ideas on opera in the French language: it is

not possible because the cadence of French is unfit for
music.[73] Nevertheless, Rousseau attempted another opera.
However, this one, Pygmalion, was a spoken drama with
instrumental accompaniment. With this work he created the
melodrama.

Rousseau's melodic concepts, that of simple, easy-
to-sing melodies looks to the classical style that was
just emerging. This is in contrast to the almost
"unending" melodies of the late Baroque. It is safe to
say that Rousseau's melodic aesthetic and Rameau's
harmonic aesthetic laid the foundation of the style that
was to grow out of the First Vienna School. Let us now
move across the Rhine and look at a musicologist who
turned to the past and transmitted the theories of
Rameau to Germany.

f. Friedrich Marpurg, 1718-1795

Marpurg is best remembered today for two things:
his book on fugue, and his polemical war with Johann
Kirnberger over fugal technique and the relative merits
of Rameau's harmonic theory. However, Marpurg did more
than write a fugue book and battle with other theorists.

He wrote and edited three music periodicals. Der
critische Musicus an der Spree (1749-1750) is devoted to
current musical topics directed to the middle-class
amateur. The Historisch-kritische Beyträge zur Aufnahme
der Musik (1754-1778) is much like the earlier publication
but is more professional in style. It contains book
reviews, biographies of famous musicians, theoretical

discussions and a whole issue (1778) devoted to tuning and
temperament. The Kritische Briefe über die Tonkunst, mit
kleinen Clavierstücken und Singoden begleitet, von einer
musikalischen Gesellschaft in Berlin (1760-1764) contains,
as the title indicates, small music pieces, but also a
collection of letters all written by Marpurg for an
imaginary Berlin music society. These letters are
polemical in nature and are directed to Kirnberger and
George A. Sorge about the fugue and Rameau's theories.
These music journals continue a tradition started by
Mattheson of disseminating musical knowledge to a wider
public than might be possible through technical books.

Marpurg's didactic works cover the area of keyboard
performance, thorough-bass and composition. One such
work is his Die Kunst das Clavier zu spielen (1762).[74]
This work is in two parts: part one deals with a
general introduction to the keyboard itself; a section
on elementary harmony and reading music; performance
practice, how to perform trills, etc.; and ends with a
section on fingering. Part two is concerned with the
art of accompaniment and the principles of figured-bass.

His monumental theoretical work is the Abhandlung
von der Fuge (1753-1754).[75] This treatise is a textbook
of fugal writing drawn primarily from the music of J. S.
Bach. As a theory of fugue based on the practice of
fugal writing, Marpurg is the first to have to come to
terms with the dichotomy between theory and practice.
His teaching is based on real music. Yet, as a

scientific project, fugue must be reducible to a set of
rules, e.g., the answer is a transposition of the
subject into another key. This rule does not always
apply in real music. There is, also, a degree of free
composition in fugal literature that answers only to the
composer's fancy. To overcome this dualism between
theory and practice, Marpurg generates the rule through
a comparison of many fugues and then lists the exceptions, much as a grammar book does when reducing a
language to a set of rules. The consequences for future
generations are that Marpurg created the school-book
fugue. He helped in the divorce between the teaching of
music and compositional practice. One takes a fugue
exam to see how well one can follow the rules--never
mind the exceptions. This same didactic process has
been followed with harmony and musical form. The whole
art has been reduced to rules.

Marpurg's contributions to musicology are those of
a transmitter of a tradition, not those of a revo-
lutionary. He continued the German periodical tradition
in his journalistic endeavors, and he passed on to the
classical period and the 19th century the contrapuntal
techniques of the High Baroque.

Let us now move from the systematic side of
musicology to the beginnings of the historical. We have
seen, as far back as Plato's Laws, an interest in the
description of musical practice, but always for ahis-
torical purposes. In the later decades of the 18th
century writers on music were beginning to take an
interest in the history of music as history. The two

central figures in this historical approach are Charles
Burney and Sir John Hawkins.

g.   John Hawkins, 1719-1789

Hawkins' A General History of the Science and
Practice of Music (1776) did not spring full-blown from
the head of the muses.[76] The French encyclopédistes
were influential in the process of such a history. Some
of Hawkins' entries might well fit into an encyclopedia
of music. Up until Burney and Hawkins, Padre Martini's
Storia della Musica (1757-1781) had been the major music
history to come out of the 18th century. As we shall
see, J. N. Forkel was the first to undertake a
systematic approach to music history.

A short exposition of Sir John's "Author's
Dedication and Preface" will suffice to show the genesis
and methodology of his history.[77] Sir John tells us
that his reasons for writing such a history are his love
for music, and a wish to put years of collecting treatises and music manuscripts to practical use. He
excuses any errors in the work because of its novelty
and "the necessity he was under of making out himself
the road which he was to travel." He states the purpose
of the history as

        the investigation of the principles, and a
        deduction of the progress of the science....
        The settling music upon somewhat like a
        footing of equality with those, which...are
        termed the sister arts; to reprobate the

> vulgar notion that its ultimate end is merely
> to excite mirth; and...to demonstrate that
> its principles are founded in certain general
> and universal laws....

Pursuant to this method, Hawkins uses many
illustrations, especially of musical instruments, and
musical compositions to demonstrate stylistic characteristics and changes. He acknowledges the music of
other peoples, but cannot inquire into them because he
believes them to be unscientific. Besides which, how
are we "to know what are the sounds that most delight a
Hottentot, a wild American, or even a more refined
Chinese?" At least we have here a passing nod at what
was to become comparative musicology, i.e.,
ethnomusicology, even though he is unwilling to pursue
the topic. Finally, he includes some biographical
material and tells us why:

> For the insertions of biographical memoirs
> and characters of eminent musicians, it may
> be given as a reason, that, having benefited
> mankind by their studies, it is but just that
> their memories should live.

In other words, we remember these writers out of a sense
of duty and thankfulness for what they have given us.
Later on he qualifies that somewhat sentimental attitude
toward biography by noting that the lives of some musicians "are in some sort a history of the arts themselves." Biography, then, is not just self-indulgence
out of duty, but can be helpful in determining the style
and history of the art.

Now for some characteristics and general
observations about the General History. As Hawkins
pointed out, its plan is chronological, ancient Greek to
his own day, but within each section there is an
unsystematic mixture of history, music theory,
organology, biography, etc. Sir John does not help his
reader in that he gives neither a table of contents nor
chapter headings to serve as subject guides. The work
is arranged in five volumes of four books of ten
chapters each--but this is of no help when it comes to
subject matter. At least an index was added in the 19th
century! One amusing section deals with the effect of
music on animals.[78] One English pundit published a
parody of this section which is entitled "The Wonderful
Power of Musick in its Effects on Mice & Spiders."

One last point differentiates Hawkins from his
Enlightened contemporaries. He was much more interested
in antique music than they. He was interested in this
music for its own sake and not as a curiosity from the
past. He was not a slave to the idea of eternal musical
progress. He found much of the music of his day to be
"noise and clamour." As he writes:

> we may impute the gradual declination from
> the practice and example of the ablest
> proficients in harmony, discoverable in the
> compositions of the present day, which, as
> they abound in noise and clamour, are totally
> void of energy.[79]

His final word is to write that this music is
"constructed without art or elegance."

It is unavoidable that Hawkins is compared with his
countryman and fellow music historian Charles Burney
whose General History of Music came out in the same year
as that of Hawkins. These two histories are neither
redundant nor contradictory, but complementary of each
other. Burney is not as interested in older music and
goes into more detail about Continental music in the
18th century than does Hawkins. Burney is easier to
read in that his history is better organized than
Hawkins'. Both works are necessary for an understanding
of the beginnings of the musical historian's methods and
purposes.80

We must now cross the Narrow Seas and on to Germany
for a look at the first systematic and codified attempts
at what was to become modern musicology.

§ 7.   J. N. Forkel (1749-1818) and the first attempt at codification

With Forkel we come to the end of the Age of
Reason and feel the first stirrings of the romantic mood
that was to engulf Europe in the 19th century. Nowhere
is this romantic feeling more evident than in his
biography of J. S. Bach (1802).81 Forkel's reasons for
writing this biography are not only artistic but also
nationalistic. Individuality and nationalism are part
of the romantic spirit and Forkel appeals to the
Germanness of his audience in his preface: "For Bach's
works are a priceless national patrimony; no other
nation possesses a treasure comparable to it." A
publisher in Leipzig had proposed a complete edition of

Bach's works and Forkel responded with this biography in
order to kindle national pride in a native son. "I deem
it a duty to remind the public of this obligation and to
kindle interest in it in every German heart. To that
end these pages appear...." And, finally, "not merely
the interests of music but our national honour are
concerned to rescue from oblivion the memory of one of
Germany's greatest sons."[82] So, this biography is in
reality an encomium rather than a critical study of
Bach's life and works. Biography, as we understand it,
was going to have to wait until the middle of the 19th
century to come to full flower with G. N. Nissen's life
of Mozart (1828) and the monumental life of Palestrina
by G. Baini (1828).

One of the more important of Forkel's contributions
is in the area of bibliography: he founded the art. In
1792 he published his _Allgemeine Litteratur der Musik_.[83]
The bibliography is of books on music (no scores) and is
divided into two large sections: History of Music, and
Theory and Practice of Music. The subtitle of the
bibliography is descriptive of the work:

> Introduction to the knowledge of musical
> books, which have been written from the
> earliest to the latest times amongst the
> Greeks, Romans and the most recent European
> nations.[84]

There are around 3000 annotated entries covering the
ancients to the writers of the 1790's. Each part is
systematically arranged by topic and the entries in
these subsections are alphabetically arranged. A

typical entry, under the subsection "Instructions to, in
particular, choral singing" is:

Zabern (Iacobus); Ars bene cantandi choralen
cantus Moguntiae, 1500. 12. s. Theoph. Sin-
ceri Nachr. von alten und raren Büchern,
St.VI. S.337 wo dieses Werk beurtheilt wird.

Forkel set the standard for all subsequent music
bibliographies in his systematic arrangement and the
clarity of the entries. He projected a companion volume
for musical scores but did not complete the work.

He also projected a music history from the
beginnings of music down to his own day. However,
during the writing of the section on the 16th century
came the call to write the homage to Bach and he never
finished the history. The Allgemeine Geschichte der
Musik (1788, 1801) is the first large-scale German
attempt since the histories of Burney and Hawkins.[85]

Forkel's history is also systematic in that it is
chronological and topical. In the introduction he gives
the reader all the possible musical and extra-musical
topics that he will cover in the work.[86] He discusses
such topics as the origins of melody (he compares it to
that of language), harmony and rhythm (§ 32); notation
(§ 58); criticism (§ 121); and ends with a schema of
musical rhetoric (§ 134). The first volume, after this
introduction, starts with a discussion of the origins of
music. He believes music to be innate in man and as
much a part of his being as language. Then comes his
chronological-topical exposition beginning with the

Egyptians. He follows through Hebrew, Greek (196
sections) and Roman music. He ends vol. 1 with Boëthius
and Cassiodorus.

Volume 2 opens with a long (§ 1-74) discussion of
church music in general. Chapter I takes church music
down to the death of Gregory the Great. Chapter II goes
from Gregory's death to Guido of Arezzo. This chapter
demonstrates Forkel's interest in cultural history and a
belief, unlike that of earlier historians, that all
facets of the human experience interpenetrate each other
and that one cannot isolate phenomena and do scientific-
historical justice to such phenomena. He opens this
chapter with a section on the European political climate
of the 10th century. This is followed with a section on
science and art in the hands of the religious. He also
covers purely musical topics as in § 38, which is on
scales: "Von Gamma und Gamm=ut." The history ends with
Franchino Gafori. Forkel's musical aesthetics is at
work in this history as an attempt at universal music
history. Music, for Forkel, was man's means of
expressing human emotion and feeling, much in the same
way that language is man's means of expressing ideas and
concepts. He could not accept the 18th-century idea of
music as mere enjoyment and pastime.

For our project, Forkel's major contribution is his
endeavor to codify and systematize musical knowledge in
the small volume Ueber die Theorie der Musik, insofern
sie Liebhabern und kennern nothwendig und nützlich ist
(1777).[87] Forkel is using the term "theory" not in the
sense of music theory, but in a critico-scientific
manner. His object is to systematize the study of music

in so far as it will be useful to amateurs and
connoisseurs. He is standing back from the wealth of
musical knowledge and attempting to bring classificatory
order out of chaos. One might go so far as to say that
he is doing metamusic.

Echoing John Locke, Forkel tells us that the human
mind is a blank page <u>leeres</u> <u>Blatt</u> on which, little by
little, concepts and knowledge are written by Nature.
So it is with art and science--we learn it all from
Nature. But man discovers order in nature and
promulgates this order in the form of laws and rules.
The mind arranges the gifts of Nature, which are given
in an haphazard fashion.[88] Art and music, being part of
the natural order, are also governed by laws and rules.
Forkel has taken it upon himself to systematize this
gift of Nature--man's language of the emotions <u>Sprache</u>
<u>der</u> <u>Empfindungen</u>.[89]

The resultant system is complete and is still
considered the basis for all modern musicologies; the
system itself has never been fundamentally questioned.
As Wolf Franck writes: "basically his system, from the
beginning, accounted for everything musicology has ever
claimed as its subject matter."[90]

There are, according to Forkel, five major
divisions in this science of music (it will be left to a
later writer to call it "musicology"): physical acoustics, mathematical acoustics, musical grammar (notation
and theory), musical rhetoric (form and style), music
criticism (aesthetics and performance practice).[91] One
major aspect of modern musicology <u>seems</u> to be missing

from this schema: historical musicology. History, for
Forkel, is the basic assumption for there being this
theory of music; music unfolds itself historically. As
Franck points out, "history is...nothing but the gradual
revelation of the nature of music in the course of time
and is therefore completely contained in his system."[92]
What this means is that one can do a history of any one
of the divisions mentioned or any of the subsections,
e.g., the history of notation, the history of music
theory, the history of performance practice, etc.

In sum: Forkel lived and worked in an age of
change, the change from the universalism of the Age of
Reason to the individualism of Romanticism. He stood at
the threshold of the Industrial Revolution and the
scientification of all knowledge. Nature is to be
objectified and music with it--not music qua heard
music, but music documents: scores, treatises,
histories, theories, etc. He objectified the study of
music in its paper existence. He set musicology on an
objective scientific high road that it has followed well
into the 20th century and few have dared to take to the
footpaths.

We have so far travelled in this chapter from
Descartes to Forkel, from the mid-1600's to 1800. We must
stop and cast a glance over our shoulders and see where we
have been so that we can better understand where we shall
travel in the 19th century.

The impression gained when reading the works of
these Enlightened musicologists is twofold: constant
acceleration in the use of scientific methods and

increased specialization arising from various musical
schemata. The first breakthrough was that of Sauveur
and his mathematizing physical acoustics which had the
effect of a new grounding for music theory. From this
point on the matrix from which nearly all theoretical
questions arose and answers were proffered would be
acoustics and not pure mathematics.

   The age was also an age of encyclopedias and the
urge to try and universalize the art was strong.
Mersenne's Harmonie Universelle is such an attempt.
Mattheson had an encyclopedic mind that harkened to the
voice of the Age of Reason, studied the ancients, and
reintroduced the scientific ideas of Aristoxenus into
mainstream musicology. Mattheson was also thorough in
his use of Cartesian methods in his music theory.

   With Rameau, we have an open avowal of the desire
to formulate a theory of harmony based on scientific
models. He even admits to reading Descartes' Discourse
on Method and consciously applying the method to the
demonstration of the generation of harmony. Such
methods are evidence that one must do more than just
listen to music: one must reason to discover principles. From a combination of Sauveur's mathematical
acoustics and Cartesian method, Rameau reduces harmonic
theory to the concept of functional harmony.

   With Rousseau, musicology advanced in the art of
lexicography in the style of the encyclopédie. All
subsequent music dictionaries look to Rousseau's as the
paradigm.

The scientific search for rules entered into the
area of composition with Marpurg's fugue book. Marpurg
set in motion a trend of developing hybrid examples from
actual music. These hybrids have, in many cases, taken
on a life of their own in the academic situation.

Music historiography has its beginning in the mid-
1700's. With writers like Hawkins and Burney, even
though their histories might be termed anecdotal in
nature, we see a trend that culminates in the highly
systematic history of Forkel and his musicological
progeny.

Finally, Forkel has given us the first systematic
codification of all musical knowledge since the
ancients, not only a theoretical basis in his Ueber die
Theorie, but in two practical applications of this
theory, the Allgemeine Litteratur der Musik and the
Allgemeine Geschichte der Musik, both of which are conceived in the universal manner of the Enlightenment.
Forkel has also given us the bare beginnings of
biography in his book on J. S. Bach. This work is in no
sense a criticosystematic study, as later biographies
were to be, but an encomium.

The Age of Reason gave to the 19th century an
heightened interest and belief in the progress of
scientific knowledge in general and music in particular.
The 19th century will spin out this web of scientific
belief until all human experience is caught in it.

§ 8. Nineteenth-century movements
toward musicology

This penultimate section of our retrospective of
musicology might begin with questions--questions of
opposites, possible paradoxes. What is the effect of
the Romantic movement on the scientific projects of the
previous century? How are science and Romanticism to be
combined? What is the result of that union? The
intellectual climate at the start of the 19th century
was in the full optimism of the tightly constructed
metaphysical system of Hegel, yet it ended in the
disillusioned laughter of Nietzsche. Between Hegel and
Nietzsche events took place that reshaped the world
politically and scientifically. All these events were
tinged with what Schiller termed a constant yearning for
etwas mehr. It is in this yearning for the past and the
future tempered by science that musicology was finally
shaped and given to the 20th century.

a. François-Joseph Fétis, 1784-1871

The Belgian musicologist and composer Fétis worked
and wrote in nearly all areas of interest to music
scholars and made important contributions, especially in
music lexicography. In the area of music theory he
wrote a nonacademic fugue and counterpoint book, the
Traité du contrepoint et de la fugue (1824)[93] and
several harmony books, most notably the Traité complet
de la théorie et de la practique de l'harmonie (1844).[94]
For a retrospective of musicology this work is important
as it represents a departure from the style of theory

that we have seen so far, i.e., mathematical or
acoustical. Fétis rejected the Rationalists' notion
that harmony is based on natural laws and therefore is
universal in character. It is society, human beings,
that order sound into melodies, scales and harmonies.
This ordering process is based on the Zeitgeist of the
historical epoch in question. Thus, differences in
musical practice are anthropologically based, not
founded in Nature. Within his harmonic theory, Fétis
coined the term "tonality" to describe the relationship
that exists between one tone and the tonic, and also,
that it is something that can be retained in memory.[95]
This magnetism between notes and chords had been noticed
and queried by many theorists starting with Aristotle.[96]
This musical magnetism now has a name: tonality.

In the field of lexicography, the Biographie
Universelle des Musiciens et bibliographie générale de
la Musique (1834-1844), is one of the most comprehensive
music biographical dictionaries of the 19th century and
is still a standard reference work, especially for 19th-
century French musicians. In the preface to the 2nd
edition (1868) Fétis describes the two points of view
one can take toward the history of music, the second of
which is the value of the work of artists and the part
each has played in the development and transformation of
the art.[97] Later in the same preface he writes that he
hopes that the dictionary will clarify the style current
in the 18th century as they set the stage for the music
of the 19th century.[98]

In the genre of music history, Fétis started but
never finished his Histoire générale de la Musique

(1869).[99] From the very first sentence of the preface
we know that he had a different attitude toward the
history of music than his predecessors. He tells us
that the history of music is inseparable from the
understanding of the special qualities of the people
that cultivate the art. This should come as no great
surprise in view of his harmonic theories. He also
questions the use of geometrical theories in the service
of music and a natural scale that is supposed to be the
basis for all music.[100] Also, he does not subscribe to
the Enlightenment ideas of musical progress and the idea
that all non-Western music is inferior because it has
not progressed as far as Western music and that it is
incapable of systematization. In the preface to his
Biographie Universelle he writes: "One of the greatest
obstacles to the fairness of judgments on the value of
musical works is found in the doctrine of progress
applied to the arts."[101] He maintained that the arts
merely change, not move in some evolutionary progression.[102] We see here a Romantic shift in emphasis from
the Rationalist belief in the universality of Natural
Law being reflected in music and its progress to the
idea that music changes and that the music of the past
could be greater than that of the present. This logical
possibility opened the musical past to musicological
study where before it had been a closed book, or at
least a book that most music scholars cared not to open.

The belief in change, not progress, led to a
genuine, not just antiquarian, interest in music of the
past. In the case of Fétis, this interest was in the
Renaissance. The peculiar character of his Renaissance
research was that it was objective, yet laced with a

subjective yearning for the past that is so characteristic of the Romantics. From this union, scientific
objectivity and romantic yearning for the etwas mehr
buried in the past, modern musicology was born.[103]

   Following through on his humanist beliefs about the
origins and growth of music, and that one cannot divorce
music history form geography, anthropology, ethnology
and linguistics,[104] Fétis opens his history of music
with a long study of non-European musics. He has
initiated what was to become comparative musicology or
ethnomusicology.[105] In the course of these
ethnomusicological studies he discusses folk-type music,
religious music, music theory, organology, etc., all
accompanied with many musical and organological illustrations. By the time the reader has reached the end
of volume I he has gone through the music of the ancient
Hebrews. So monumental a task was left unfinished by
Fétis. He wrote five volumes but got only as far as the
15th century.

   Aside from the wealth of material in these five
volumes, the work's importance lies in the philosophy of
music history that guided it. He wanted to show the
sequence of historical events as the change of music
itself. To that end he eliminated all biographical data
from the history. For such material one can always have
recourse to the Biographie Universelle.

   Finally, Fétis delved into didactics. He wrote two
books dealing with pedagogy: Méthode des Méthodes de
Chant[106] and a companion work Méthode des Méthodes de
Piano.[107] These two works are an inventory of didactic

writings on singing and the piano, all done with a
practical end: teaching singing and piano. The piano
method contained older music in an attempt to teach
virtuous older music and not just that of the 19th
century. Fétis also wanted performers to learn
performing techniques of the past in order to give more
authentic performances of older music. One "innovation"
suggested by Fétis is that there is no good reason why
pianists should not use thumbs on black keys when necessary. Fétis knew that this was common in the 17th and
18th centuries. The volume contains not only this
material on performance of older music, but technical
studies including three études by Chopin and pieces by
Liszt and Mendelssohn.

b. Moritz Hauptmann, 1792-1868

While most music theory, at least from the
Renaissance to Hauptmann's time, was a search for the
grounding of musical law in the natural sciences,
Hauptmann looked to an earlier age for a single law that
permeates the whole art. He was looking for that single
principle that would account for all music, in much the
same way as pre-Socratic philosophy was a search for a
unitary cosmic principle. Through the application of
Hegelian dialectics, Hauptmann discovered what he
thought was that principle. In his book, Die Natur de
harmonik und Metrik, (1853) he enunciates this law as
"unity, with the opposite of itself, and the removal of
the opposite: immediate unity, which through an element
of being at two with itself passes into mediated
unity."[108]

Nearly all music theories from the time of Sauveur have been based on the acoustical properties of the partial series. Hauptmann rightly noticed that in the harmonic series the pitches 7, 11, 13, and 14 are not "in tune" with common intonation practice. The first b-flat is far too flat, the f too sharp and the a too flat for our intonation system. From this he concludes that "this necessitates modification of the degrees in question; they must be raised and lowered, whereby occasion is taken for speaking of the difference between a natural system of notes and an artificial one, as of the difference between a savage condition and a civi- lised."[109] From this juxtaposition of savage sound and civilised harmony, he finds nothing but absurdity and the need for endless justifications of harmonic theo- ries. Instead of reworking the current theories, which he thinks are wrong, he starts with the civilized scale and searches for the harmonic principles that guide the progression of tones, that something called tonality by Fétis and for which Aristotle had no answer. He turned to Hegel for the answer.

The basic Hegelian idea of a clash of opposites and resolution of opposition, only to give rise to more opposition has been applied to many areas and it is not surprising that someone should explain the tonic- dominant relationship in Hegelian terms. In Hauptmann's hands Hegel's thesis becomes simplicity or unity (the octave), antithesis becomes division or separation (the fifth) and synthesis becomes reconcilement or restored unity (the major third) which is a mediated unity. All harmony and meter are related to this governing princi- ple.[110] Within harmony, tones, keys, triads,

dissonance, etc. are all related to this key
dialectical concept.

Let us look at how this works in the area of
harmony. There are only three unchangeable, directly
intelligible intervals: I. The Octave (unity); II.
The Fifth (opposition); and III. The Major Third
(mediated unity). These three intervals, when united,
become a triad, which is a double-sided idea: positive
(major) and negative (minor).[111] Hauptmann denotes the
triad in this fashion: I-III-II. Thus, the C major
triad becomes:[112]

$$I - III - II$$
$$C \quad e \quad\quad G$$

This configuration can give rise, in Hegelian fashion,
to other dialectical relationships:[113]

$$I - III - II$$
$$C \quad e \quad\quad G \quad\quad b \quad\quad D$$
$$I \quad - \quad III - II$$
$$\langle I - III - II \rangle$$

Here the "G" has a dual function either as antithesis or
as thesis. The dialectic set off thus <> does not seem
to occur in Hauptmann although it would be more genuine
Hegelianism where the synthesis would generate a new
thesis, etc. More than likely this would not occur
musically because it would overemphasize the third
relationship, while it is the fifth relationship that is
the source of harmonic tension or the feeling of
tonality. Let Hauptmann have the last word:

>To understand such a schema rightly, let it
>be observed once for all, that by the symbol
>I-II is expressed, not a first and second,
>but the standing apart of opposite determina-
>tions, and by III, not a third or triple, but
>the coming together of the same.[114]

Hauptmann's musical theories will have an impact on
later theorists, especially those who also question the
use of the natural overtone series as a ground for
harmonic theory. Hugo Riemann, most notably, will use
Hauptmann's ideas, coupled with those of Rameau, and
bring to completion the idea of functional harmony.
However, Riemann thought of Hauptmann as working in a
theoretical vacuum, whereas Riemann wanted to take this
dialectical schema and devise a system of harmonic
understanding and musical logic from musical practice
itself.[115]

                c. August Ambros, 1816-1876

     The Austrian musicologist Ambros has given us two
works that enhanced two areas in musicology: aesthetics
and music history. Ambros wrote his aesthetic book Die
Grenzen der Musik und Poesie[116] in 1856 as a more pro-
gressive answer to the aesthetic conservatism of Eduard
Hanslick's Vom Musikalisch-schönen written in 1854.[117]
Hanslick's fundamental thesis is to refute the view that
aesthetics be founded on feelings and emotions, and
ground it objectively, i.e., scientifically, instead.

> Any such investigation <aesthetics> will
> prove utterly futile unless the method
> obtaining in natural science be followed, at
> least in the sense of dealing with the things
> themselves, in order to determine what is
> permanent and objective in them....[118]

The aspect of Hanslick's theory that Ambros was
objecting to the most was Hanslick's conclusion that the
only proper music is instrumental music and that words,
that is a text, have no place in music proper. Words are
always subjectively tinged, for Hanslick; thus when
coupled with music, that music is not capable of objective
elucidation.

Ambros, on the other hand, does not see the need
for such a scientifically objective aesthetics for music
because his fundamental attitude is Hegelian, i.e.,
dialectical and progressivistic in the sense of the
historical methods of Jacob Burkhardt. Music belongs to
the human realm not to that studied by the Naturwissenschaften. Ambros' task, then, is to

> establish on fixed principles the points at
> which the domains of both <poetry and music>
> touch; where in touching they coincide, and
> where there is between them no point of
> contact whatever.[119]

At the end of the preface to his aesthetics he singles
out Hanslick as his aesthetic opponent who he will
"often dispute" in his work.[120]

The importance of Ambros' unfinished music history,
the Geschichte der Musik (1862), lies in his attempt to
do a cultural history at the same time as a music
history.[121] For Ambros, music does not exist in splendid isolation from the other arts; they all developed
together. All the arts belong to a cultural complex and
develop in an Hegelian fashion playing off each other.
An example of this cultural approach to music history is
in the third book, on ancient music, where Ambros
devotes a section to the historical situation of the
ancient Greeks and the "astronomical symbolism of Greek
music, its political and ethical meaning."[122] With
Ambros' history the attitudes toward music history
became less and less insular, and subsequent writers
would have to take music more in its cultural setting as
a cultural phenomenon to be expounded in a cultural
context.

d.   Hermann von Helmholtz, 1821-1894

Let us now move back to the systematic side of the
emerging musicological schema. As we do so, it might be
wise to look back at the varieties of music theories
and try to classify them as to approach or methodology.
Doing this will better place Helmholtz in the order of
systematic musicology.

Five basic approaches to music theory can be
discerned from the retrospective so far. First, music
theory based on pure mathematics held sway from the
ancients (except for Aristoxenus) through the Late Middle
Ages. This approach uses mathematics to explain either

imagined or heard intervalic relationships. Second, with
the work of the 18th-century acoustician, Sauveur, and the
music theoretician, Rameau, we have an harmonic theory
based on mathematical acoustics; that is, the heard
partials expressed mathematically. The 19th century
produced two new approaches to music theory. First, there
is that of Fétis, which is humanistic in approach. In
this method music is seen as a creation and function of
culture or society and must be analyzed in that context.
Second, there is that of Moritz Hauptmann, who noticed
tuning discrepancies in the harmonic series and so decided
to abandon mathematical acoustics as an organizing
principle for harmony and an explanation for tonality.
Hauptmann applied the dialectical principles of Hegel as
the locus for an analysis of harmony and meter. Fifth,
Helmholtz attempts a new grounding of harmonic theory on
physiological acoustics. Thus, there are five approaches
to music theory: pure mathematics, mathematical
acoustics, humanistic-cultural, musical dialectics, and
physiological acoustics. In the first, second, fourth and
fifth approaches musical logic is external to the music,
being imposed on harmony by mathematics, the natural
partial series, otological principles and society. Only
in the third method do we find musical logic internally
generated by the juxtaposition of octave, fifth and third:
the system creates its own logic.

Helmholtz worked in many areas of scientific
research other than acoustics, e.g., neurology, color-
blindness, theory of fluids and electricity. There are
two works that deal with acoustics. The work on the
physiology of the ear Die Mechanik der Gehörknöchelchen
und des Trommelfells (1869) is a full study of the

anatomical, physiological and mathematical aspects of the
workings of the inner ear.[123] Helmholtz was interested,
in this work, in how sound is transmitted by the bones of
the ear.

His most important work, for our purposes, is his
Die Lehre von den Tonempfindungen als physiologische
Grundlage für die Theorie der Musik (1863).[124] Let
Helmholtz introduce his work:

> In the present work an attempt will be made
> to connect the boundaries of two sciences,
> which, although drawn towards each other by
> many natural affinities, have hitherto
> remained practically distinct--I mean the
> boundaries of physical and physiological
> acoustics on the one side, and of musical
> science and esthetics on the other.[125]

He goes on to tell us that he is not dealing with
rational nor affectational connections in the question
of harmonic progress (tonality) or interval generation,
but with the "natural power of immediate sensation,"
the datum sound.[126] It will be much easier to do this
with music than any other art because "music stands in a
much closer connection with pure sensation than any of
the other arts." Painting is an exception in so far as
it deals with pure color. Language is also sound, but
it is the meaning and affectational aspects of language
that we are immediately aware of, not pure sound as in
most music.

Helmholtz's aim is a physiological acoustics based
on the investigation of the "processes that take place in
the ear itself."[127] From this otology he hopes to devise
an explanation for the sensation of dissonance, consonance
and tonality. To that end On the Sensation of Tone is
divided into three sections: part I deals with the
physical and physiological aspects of how we hear
harmonics, or more than one tone at a time, what Helmholtz
calls combination tones; part II treats further of the
disturbances created, dissonance-consonance, by these
combination tones (dissonance is caused by a clash of
beats, this reminds one of Galileo's explanation of
dissonance); and part III is his system of harmony based
on his physiological findings.

His basic conclusion is that the "physiological
properties of the sensation of hearing exercise a direct
influence on the construction of a musical system."[128]
He comes out on the side of those who believe that the
harmonic system we have developed is directly related to
the overtone series, whose operation is grounded in
natural law. Triads are the natural basis for harmony,
e.g., C-E-G is natural because "G" and "E" are part of
"C" in the overtone series. Thus, Helmholtz has created
an acoustically based harmonic theory, but one built on
physiology and not pure mathematics.

e. Robert Eitner, 1832-1905

Robert Eitner was music's 19th-century
bibliographer. Although he wrote many articles on
musicological subjects, his most important contributions

were two monumental bibliographies. Let us consider
them in order of publication.

His Bibliographie der Musik-Sammelwerke des XVI.
und XVII. Jahrhunderts (1877), written in collaboration
with Haberl, Lagerberg and Pohl is a bibliography of
music collections printed in the 16th and 17th
centuries.[129] The work is arranged in chronological
order (date of publication) and gives the location of
copies. It also contains extensive indexes: composer,
title, first line of text, publisher, etc. In the
foreword to the bibliography Eitner gives us a short
history of such bibliographies starting with that of
Petrucci (1498).[130] This work of Eitner is the model
for all such subsequent bibliographies.

In 1871 Eitner began another bibliographical
project[131] that was not published until 1900-1904:
Biographisch-Bibliographisches Quellen-Lexikon der
Musiker und Musikgelehrten der christlichen Zeitrechnung
bis zur Mitte des neunzehnten Jahrhunderts, better known
as the Quellen-Lexikon.[132] Eitner believes that bibliography is the foundation for any historical knowledge
and music is no exception. The music historian would be
lost in his scholarly pursuit without reliable bibliographies as a guide to the mass of literature in his
field. Eitner was well aware of the work of Fétis and
others, but these bibliographies gave neither biographical information nor the location of source material.
Eitner's intention is to fill this need with a Source-
Dictionary, biographically arranged.[133] Eitner set two
limitations to his bio-bibliography: the Christian era

and no individual born after 1780 is included, giving him a cut-off date of approximately 1840.[134] Each entry contains a very short biographical sketch and a union-list of works. The ten volumes of this set records the manuscript and printed music holdings of over 200 European libraries.

Eitner also engaged in two other publication projects: one a journal, and the other a series of previously unpublished early music and music books. In 1869 he began publishing the journal Monatshefte für Musikgeschichte. In 1873 he began work on the 29-volume series Publikationen Älterer Praktischer und Theoretischer Musikwerke.

f. Hermann Kretzschmar, 1848-1924

While the Low Countries produced Fétis as their musical humanist, German humanism produced Kretzschmar. Music was a human-created phenomenon for Kretzschmar, and its history a history of culture, not the history of an isolated art form. Thus, musicology is the project of uncovering the complex of relationships that exist between a work of art, the artist and the cultural milieu. He called his method "musical hermeneutics" and conceived of it as part of a broader cultural history and a method within the nest of Geisteswissenschaften and Kunstwissenschaften.

The ground of this style of musicology comes from his humanistic schooling, the study of ancient languages and related exegetical problems and his belief that

music is a performing art--all else being peripheral.
The cornerstone of Kretzschmar's musicology was his
attitude that the methods used to explain the art must
be generated by and comform to the art, not the art
to the theory-method.

In an essay entitled "Anregungen zur Förderung
musikalischer Hermeneutik" (1902) Kretzschmar outlines
the aims of his style of musicology.[135] Hermeneutics
comes from bible exegesis, and was very early taken over
by the Geisteswissenschaften and Kunstwissenschaften, the
object being the same in both sciences: to investigate
the meaning and thought content <Ideengehalt>, the form,
and above all to search for the soul of the work in
every utterance with the final aim of gaining the pure
core of thought <reinen Gedankenkern> that generated the
work.[136] In another place he gives the hermeneutical
project as a method of dissociating the emotions from
the notes and to verbalize its development.

Kretzschmar, because of his musical hermeneutics,
was very interested in music education and pedagogy. He
wanted to take the study and science of music out of the
lecture halls and make such knowledge available to a
wider musical public. To that end he wrote two series
of books: Führer durch den Konzertsaal (1888-1890)[137]
and the Kleine Handbücher der Musikgeschichte nach
Gattungen.[138]

g. Hugo Riemann, 1849-1919

After having read law, philosophy, and history at
the University of Berlin, Riemann took the doctorate in
philosophy from the University of Göttingen (1873).
There were no areas of study in music--whether practical
or theoretical--that did not receive attention from
Riemann's eclectic mind. The areas that are the most
important for this study are musicology in general,
music history, music theory and lexicography.

In 1908 he published a little volume entitled
Grundriss der Musikwissenschaft.[139] It is best that we
start with this work as it outlines Riemann's attitudes
and beliefs about the purpose and scope of musicology.
Musicology must ground all musical knowledge through the
use of two basic scientific areas: the exact sciences
of mathematics and mechanics, and the pure science of
the Geisteswissenschaften. From the former will come
acoustical knowledge as the study of sound itself and
the physiology of hearing. From the latter musicology
will take advantage of philosophy, logic, and aesthetics
and the human studies in general. The bridge between
the two basic areas, mathematical sciences and human
studies, is to be psychology as the study of human
experience and the life of the soul.[140] After this
introduction, the work follows with sections on acoustics, tone physiology and psychology, music aesthetics,
music theory and music history.

Riemann published, among other music histories, a
Kleines Handbuch der Musikgeschichte mit Periodisierung
nach Stil prinzipien und Formen in 1908.[141] His purpose

in writing such a history of music was his belief that
anyone who claims to have some musical knowledge must
know the history of the art and the best approach, on a
pedagogical level, is through style and form analysis.
To this end he lauds the work of other musicologists
being done in the critical and monumental editions of
the music of older masters as an aid to the study of
music and not just for the glory of musicology
itself.[142] Riemann's little handbook has the following
format: a general style period is discussed, e.g., the
music of antiquity. This is then honed down to ancient
Greek music. Then follows a bibliography of the subject
and a chronology of the history of ancient Greek music.
This same process is repeated for all major style
periods up through the 19th century.[143]

     Remaining in the historical mode, Riemann wrote one
of the first histories of notation: Studien zur
Geschichte der Notenschrift.[144] Riemann's reasoning
behind such a study is twofold: most music historians
do not deal with notation and this work is meant to fill
that gap; and the development of music theory, harmony,
counterpoint and form are all interrelated with the
problems inherent in the notation of music, e.g., the
complexity of Western counterpoint would not have
developed without an adequate notation.[145] Riemann
considers the three main types of notational symbols:
letter notations, neumes, and notes.

     In the field of systematic musicology Riemann wrote
numerous books and articles. Three of these will suffice to give an adequate representation of his music
theory. His work in systematic musicology can be

divided into two areas: the history of music theory,
and music theory proper, which would include many
didactic works on composition, counterpoint, harmony,
etc.

In his work on music theory proper, Riemann's
objective was to combine the latest knowledge in physiological acoustics and pure music theory. He states his
case in his Die Natur der Harmonik:

> Scientific investigation in the domain of
> music concerns itself, primarily, with ascer-
> taining the laws which govern sounding
> bodies, and is thus a department of physics;
> i.e., the science of acoustics. Then, pur-
> suing tones still further, and inquiring into
> the effects they produce on the human ear,
> and the mode in which those effects are pro-
> duced, it becomes a special department of
> physiology. Finally, concerning itself with
> tone perception, with the mental effects of
> these acoustic and physiological phenomena,
> and with the mental connections and relations
> of the sensations produced by sound it enters
> the domain of psychology. Out of the results
> of scientific investigation in all three
> fields of physics, physiology, and psychol-
> ogy, we get the elements of an exact theory
> of the nature of harmony.[146]

His music theory is fully developed in the book
Vereinfachte Harmonielehre, oder die Lehre von den
Tonalen Funktionen der Akkorde.[147] This theory is a

move away from the thorough-bass principles of harmony
of the previous century and toward one of chord
functions. His theory of functional harmony comes from
a synthesis of hints by Rameau, Fétis' concept of
tonality and its antecedents and Hauptmann's musical
dialectics. Chord dialectics and the "feeling" for
tonality (supported by physics, physiology and psychology), are spun out into a theory of chord dependencies.
The logic of the system dictates that the tonic (I)
chord is dependent upon its dominant (V) and its subdominant (IV) for its function as tonic or tonal center.
Also, all other chords can be related to this fundamental functional dialectic. Riemann also applied similar
principles to meter and rhythm, all based on stress
points of beats and groups of beats. This leads into a
theory of music phrase structure which is based on a
linguistic model of punctuation.

In order completely to support his music theory
Riemann undertook to write a history of music theory,
and his Geschichte der Musiktheorie im IX.-XIX.
Jahrhundert was published in 1898.[148] To date, this is
still the most comprehensive study of the subject of the
development of Western music theory.

Finally, Riemann brought German music lexicography
up to date with his Musik Lexikon (1882).[149] Riemann's
intent was to write this dictionary to serve as a music
handbook.[150] The dictionary gives short and concise
entries on the life, destiny and merit of composers,
virtuosi and music teachers and contains short lists of
works.[151]

This very short survey of Riemann's works, cut
short by Ockham's razor, had to leave out numerous other
books and articles by Riemann on such topics as opera,
the figured bass, history of musical instrument,
analysis of Bach's works, organ construction, dance and
folk music, song styles, Gregorian chant, etc. Because
of the amount and quality of his output on musical
topics, musicology as we know it today would not be the
same without him.

§ 9. Guido Adler codifies musicology

"Musicology originated at the same time as the art
of music." With this sentence Adler opens his essay
"Umfang, Methode und Ziel der Musikwissenschaft."[152]
This essay is the lead article in a journal started by
Friedrich Chrysander, who has the honor of first using
the word "Musikwissenschaft" (musicology) to describe
the emerging discipline. In the preface to the
Jahrbücher für muskalische Wissenschaft (1863, 1867)
Chrysander describes this new science in the following
terms:

We call this SCIENCE in the genuine and
complete sense; and in order to indicate that
we here enter into that circle <of the sci-
ences>, (that) we do not evade its rigorous
demands, and (that) we should like to serve
it in its entire compass to our abilities, we
are issuing the annuals under the title "für
musikalische Wissenschaft." The whole area
of musical art should be considered therein,

and equally, as much as possible, not, I
hope, as one might conclude from my previous
works and even from the contents of this
first volume, with a preference for the
historical portion of the same.[153]

Adler's essay constitutes the most comprehensive,
critical and methodological study of musicology to come
out of the 19th century and musicologists always have
had to look back to it when scrutinizing the discipline.
Let us look at the major points in the essay.

Human beings have made music from time immemorial.
The first person to reflect on music-making was the first
musicologist. The birth of musical knowledge lies in the
attempt to explain and account, through classification
schemata, for "the organic relationships of several
notes." Pythagoras' application of a mathematical schema
to notes is just such an attempt. The task of musicology
is not absolute, because the subject matter of musicology,
music, is always in a state of flux and the study of it
changes "with the state of the art of music." The
fundamental project of musicology is to "fix, determine,
and clarify musical material."[154] As the art of music
grows and changes so does the science of musicology, and
it must always "take works of art above all as a
foundation for research."

The factors entailed in such research and its
process are given in a research model which answers the
question of how musicologists might approach a piece of
music scientifically. First, the musicologist will give
a notational (paleographic) description of the work, and

if necessary a transcription into modern notation. Once
this has been done he will then proceed to answer a
whole group of questions surrounding the construction of
the piece: meter, rhythm, tonality, modality, polyphonic description, thematic development, etc. Third,
if the work is texted, he will examine the text as a
separate entity, then in its relationship to the music
vis-à-vis text-underlay, word-painting, etc. Fourth, if
the piece is purely instrumental, he must investigate
and describe the instrumentation and then the perform-
ability of the music. Once this has been accomplished,
he can start to ask questions of a stylistic nature and
also to determine the chronological placement of the
piece. Sixth, and last, he must investigate the
aesthetics of the music, its "mood content" which is the
"keystone of critical observation."[155] In the case of
aesthetic considerations, the musicologist will be on
shaky ground because of the sometimes "futile effort to
convert the mood content into words." Adler qualifies
these aesthetic statements as "scientific" because of
his belief in the essentially affective nature of music
and for musicology to be rigorous it must account for
all the parameters of the musical experience, even those
difficult to verbalize. "It will be a bold undertaking
to express scientifically the analogy of the mood contents as befits the text and the music..." It is even
bolder with non-texted music. One is reminded of
Plato's Philebus (56a) where he writes of music "that
the amount of uncertainty mixed up in it is great...."

For Adler, the primary function of aesthetics is
axiological in that there is a nest of questions the
aesthetician will attempt to answer that are evaluative

in nature. For example: What is musically beautiful?
Must every work of art be beautiful? What are the
criteria for beauty in general? These questions lead,
for Adler, to a more comprehensive matrix of determina-
tions that make up the aesthetics of music. They are:
a) the generation and effect of music; b) the relationship of music to nature; c) the relationship of music to
culture, climate, etc.; d) the classification of music
according to the type of origin; e) limitations of
musical expression (noise and music); f) the ethical
effects of music. This matrix of determination Adler
terms the "scientific questions." There are other
matters that fall within the domain of music aesthetics
that lie outside the purview of science: which is
"real" music, instrumental or vocal; which takes precedence, the text or the music; what is the high point
in religious music?

Thus, we have the outline of the "objects of
investigation for musicological research." The whole
edifice of Adler's scientific system grows from this
outline. "This <science> falls accordingly under two
headings, historical and systematic." There follows a
detailed account of all the possible divisions of these
two basic divisions and all the auxiliary sciences that
aid the musicological project.156 Adler's synopsis of
this discussion can be found as Appendix II in this
study.

Next, Adler discusses method; he writes that "the
method of musicological research is directed according
to the type of object to be investigated...", e.g.,
paleography. The musicologist, in this instance, will

have recourse to all the methods accessible to history,
diplomatics and paleology, all geared to the special
problems of musical notation. While the musicologist will
borrow freely from other studies, the special problem of
the art will transform those methods to meet the needs of
music. Fundamentally, the musicologist will use the
inductive method in investigating musical precepts and the
organic relationships between different epochs.

> He will extract that which is common from
> several examples, separate that which is
> different, and also make use of abstraction,
> in that individual parts of concretely given
> representations are neglected and others
> favored. Proposing hypotheses is also not
> out of the question.[157]

What Adler means is that it is not out of the question
for the musicologist to speculate concerning stylistic
and theoretical matters. An example of neglected repre-
sentations might be the lacunae in many musical manuscripts that must be hypothetically filled in by the
musicologist. He also might want to "finish" a work
from sketches left by the composer and such "findings"
would be speculative and hypothetical in nature.

Adler ends the essay with a section devoted to the
relationship between aesthetics, art, and the art
historian-critic. Art and aesthetics are, in
actuality, the same thing, i.e., they have the same
domain; it is just that the mode of presentation is
different. The artist creates; the aesthetician offers
critical interpretation of the art work. The art

historian acts as exegete and the science he practices
"will accomplish its task to the fullest extent only
when it maintains vital contact with art."[158] Constant
exposure to and experience of art works is the life-
blood of aesthetics and art criticism. One way in which
the aesthetician can be of service to art is through the
restoration and preservation of art works. The musicologist has a vital rôle to play in the preparation of
critical and performing editions of music and the
interpretation of performance practices of that
music.[159]

In these passages, even though Adler does not
explicitly say it, he writes as if the main function of
musicology is its aesthetic aspect. It is almost as if
"aesthetician" and "musicologist" are synonymous terms.
Adler does see aesthetics as a broad canopy covering
musicology's project because of aesthetics' philosophical grounding plus its mathematical, physical (studies
as sensation) and philological (hermeneutical) side.
Nevertheless, Adler stresses the need for codification
and systematization of _all_ the areas of study comprising
musicology, i.e., they need critical reflection. He
ends the essay with the hope that "the present attempt
at a unified summary of musicology <may> assist in
covering this need."[160]

A tentative answer might now be given to the
questions asked at the beginning of our retrospective of
the 19th century. The nature of the Romantic movement
had a twofold effect on the scientific projects of the
previous century: it broadened the musicological
Weltanschauung to include non-Western music. The whole

bevy of musicological methods that had been used to
investigate Western music came now to be used by the
ethnomusicologist. The result of this union, i.e., the
union of romantic yearning and scientific method, was a
much deeper appreciation of the past and its influences
on the present and the future. Western music is no
longer seen as the model by which all other music is to
be evaluated and described.[161]

NOTES FOR CHAPTER III

[1] René Descartes, Discourse on Method, trans. Elizabeth Haldane and G. R. T. Ross (Chicago: Encyclopaedia Britannica, Inc., 1952), p. 47.

[2] René Descartes, Meditations, trans. Elizabeth S. Haldane and G. R. T. Ross (Chicago: Encyclopaedia Britannica, Inc., 1952), p. 85 (Meditation III).

[3] Edmund Husserl, Crisis of European Sciences and Transcendental Phenomenology, trans. David Carr (Evanston: Northwestern University Press, 1970), p. 74, § 16.

[4] Marin Mersenne, Harmonie Universelle (Paris: S. Cramoisy, 1636-1637).

[5] Mersenne's discoveries about these relationships resulted in a mathematical formula by which one can determine the pitch of a string without hearing it. For the frequency (pitch) of a stretched string the following formula is given:

$$F = 1/2L \sqrt{x/m}$$

where F = frequency (pitch); L = length of the string; x = tension of the string; and, m = mass/cm of the string.

[6] Mersenne, Harmonie Universelle, vol. 1, pp. 89-180; vol. 2, pp. 440-442.

[7] Mersenne, Harmonicorum instrumentorum libri IV (Paris: Guillaume Baudry, 1635-1636, 1648).

[8] René Descartes, Compendium of Music, trans. Walter Robert (s.l.: American Institute of Musicology, 1964).

[9] Ibid., p. 16.

[10] Ibid., p. 15.

[11] Ibid., p. 12.

[12]Joseph Sauveur, Mémoires de l'Académie Royale des Sciences (Amsterdam: Chez Pierre Mortier, 1701-1713). There is a complete translation of these works in: Robert E. Maxham, "The Contributions of Joseph Sauveur (1653-1767) to Acoustics" (Ph.D. dissertation, Eastman School of Music, 1976).

[13]Maxham, "The Contributions of Joseph Sauveur," vol. 2, p. 26.

[14]This device is fully described in the Maxham dissertation, vol. 1, pp. 25-41.

[15]Ibid., vol. 2, pp. 15-25.

[16]Ibid., vol. 1, pp. 46-47.

[17]Ibid., vol. 2, p. 5.

[18]Ibid., vol. 2, pp. 6, 84-89.

[19]Ibid., vol. 1, pp. 94-110; vol. 2, pp. 70-80.

[20]Ibid., vol. 1, p. 96; vol. 2, pp. 73-74.

[21]Ibid., vol. 2, p. 1.

[22]Hermann Scherchen, The Nature of Music (n.p.: Henry Regnery Company, 1950), p. 15.

[23]L. von Köchel, Johann Josef Fux (Vienna: Hölder, 1972).   This volume contains a thematic index of Fux's works.

[24]Johann Josef Fux, Gradus ad Parnassum (Vienna: Joannis Petri van Ghelen, 1725).   Pages 41 through 139, p. 279, and the preface were translated by Alfred Mann as Steps to Parnassus: The Study of Counterpoint (New York: W. W. Norton & Co., Inc., 1943).

[25]Friedrich Blume, Renaissance and Baroque Music (New York: W. W. Norton & Co., Inc., 1967), p. 121.

[26]Fux, Steps to Parnassus, pp. 15-16.

[27]Johann Mattheson, Das neu eröffnete Orchestre
(Hamburg: bey Benjamin Schillers Wittwe im Thum, 1713).

[28]Ibid., p. 239. There is much more on the
doctrine of the affections in Der vollkomene
Capellmeister.

[29]Ibid., p. 300. "Ob die Music oder die Mahlerey
höher zu achten."

[30]Ibid., p. 304. "...wer hat doch den kleinen
Vögeln das Pfeiffen und Zwitschern gelehret, sie sind ja
nicht in Pythagorae Schule gewesen..."

[31]Ibid., p. 306. "Ist demnach primo loco in Gott
selbst, secundo in der eigentlichen Natur der rechte
warhaffte Ursprung der Music zu finden."

[32]Johann Mattheson, Das forschende Orchestre
(Hamburg: B. Schillers Wittwe und J. C. Kissner, 1721).

[33]Ernest Charles Harriss, "Johann Mattheson's Der
vollkomene Capellmeister: a Translation and Commentary"
(Ph.D. dissertation, George Peabody College for
Teachers, 1969), p. 1555.

[34]Harriss, Matheson, see fn. 33.

[35]Ibid., p. 1567.

[36]Mattheson, Der vollkomene Capellmeister, pt. I,
chap. 6; pt. II, chap. 8 and 14.

[37]Harriss, Matheson, pp. 468-544.

[38]Ibid., pp. 468-470.

[39]Ibid., p. 471.

[40]Ibid., p. 472.

[41]Ibid., p. 482.

[42]Ibid., p. 468.

[43]Ibid., p. 92.

[44]Johann Mattheson, Grundlage einer Ehrenpforte (Hamburg: In verlegung des Verfassers, 1740).

[45]Johann Mattheson, Exemplarische Organisten-Probe (Hamburg: Im Schiller und Kissnerischen Buchladen, 1719).

[46]Johann Mattheson, Kleine und Grosse General-Bass-Schule (Hamburg: J. C. Kissner, 1735).

[47]Mattheson, Exemplarische, p. 245f.

[48]Harriss, Mattheson, p. 1565.

[49]Jean-Philippe Rameau, Treatise on Harmony, trans. Philip Gossett (New York: Dover Publications, Inc., 1971).

[50]Ibid., p. xxiv.

[51]Ibid., p. xxxv.

[52]Arsen Ralph Papakhian, "Jean-Philippe Rameau's Demonstration du Principe de l'harmonie (1750) and Pierre Esteve's Nouvelle Découverts du Principe de l'harmonie (1752): a Translation" (M. M. thesis, Western Michigan University, 1973).

[53]Ibid., p. 15.

[54]Ibid., p. 22. What Rameau has demonstrated is the direct relationship between the mathematical (theoretical) representation of pitch relationships and the acoustical properties of pitch (harmonic series) and that both can be represented arithmetically. Pythagoras lives!

[55]Jean-Philippe Rameau, Origine des sciences, suivie d'une controverse sur le même sujet (Paris: 1762).

[56]This is a reduction of all harmonies to three "functionally" different chords (tonic, dominant and

subdominant) to which all other chords are related.
This concept was fully developed into an analytical tool
by Hugo Riemann, <u>Vereinfachte Harmonielehre</u> (London:
Augner and Co., 1893).

[57]Rameau, <u>Treatise</u>, p. 218.

[58]Rameau, <u>Demonstration</u>, p. 29.

[59]Rameau, <u>Treatise</u>, p. 141. In this example Rameau
mentions only the tonic and dominant as the source, but
later on (<u>Nouveau système</u>, p. 38) added the subdominant.
Actually he thought of the subdominant as the lower
dominant to the tonic, i.e., a fifth below, thus sub-.

[60]Rameau, <u>Treatise</u>, p. 154.

[61]Ibid., p. 155.

[62]Ibid., p. 156.

[63]Manfred F. Bukofzer, <u>Music in the Baroque Era</u>
(New York: W. W. Norton, 1947), p. 387.

[64]Jean-Jacques Rousseau, <u>Oeuvres De J. J. Rousseau</u>,
vol. 13 (Paris: Werdet et Lequien Fils, 1826), pp. 7-
20; 23-140. (Hereafter: Rousseau, <u>Projet</u>; Rousseau,
<u>Dissertation</u>).

[65]Rousseau, <u>Projet</u>, p. 7.

[66]Ibid., p. 9 and <u>Dissertation</u>, p. 57.

[67]Rousseau, <u>Projet</u>, p. 14.

[68]Rousseau, <u>Dissertation</u>, pp. 81ff.

[69]Jean-Jacques Rousseau, <u>Dictionnaire de Musique</u>,
in <u>Oeuvres complètes de J. J. Rousseau</u>, vol. 3 (Paris:
Furne et Cie., 1837), pp. 588-857. He also wrote a
dictionary of botany. It is in the same volume, pp.
420-446.

[70]Ibid., p. 588.

[71]John Hope Mason, The Indispensable Rousseau
(London: Quartet Books, 1979), p. 99. The "baroco of
the logicians" about which Rousseau writes is the
mnemonic device used to remember the disposition of
fourth mood, second figure of syllogisms: AOO-2.   "AOO"
coming from "baroco."

[72]Rousseau, Dictionnaire, p. 745.

[73]Jean-Jacques Rousseau, Lettre sur la Musique
François in Oeuvres de J. J. Rousseau, vol. 13 (Paris:
Werdet et Lequien Fils, 1826), pp. 229-285. Partially
translated in Strunk, Source Readings, pp. 636-654.

[74]Friedrich Marpurg, Die Kunst das Clavier zu
spielen (Berlin: A. Haude und Spener, 1753).

[75]Friedrich Marpurg, Abhandlund von der Fuge
(Berlin: A. Haude und J. C. Spener, 1753). There is an
English translation of this work in Alfred Mann, The
Study of Fugue (New Brunswick, N. J.:   Rutgers
University Press, 1958), pp. 142-212.

[76]John Hawkins, A General History of the Science
and Practice of Music (London: Novello, 1853; reprint
ed., New York: Dover Publications, Inc., 1963).

[77]Ibid., p. xix.

[78]Ibid., pp. 401, 835.

[79]Ibid., pp. 918-919.

[80]For a study of the relationship between Hawkins
and Burney see R. Stevenson, "The Rivals Hawkins, Burney
and Boswell," Musical Quarterly 36 (1950):   67-82.

[81]Johann Nicolaus Forkel, Johann Sebastian Bach his
life, art, and work, trans. Charles S. Terry (London:
Constable and Co., Ltd., 1920).

[82]Ibid., xxv-xxvi.

[83]Johann Nicolaus Forkel, <u>Allgemeine</u> <u>Litteratur</u> <u>der</u>
<u>Musik</u> (Leipzig: 1792; reprint ed., Hildesheim: Georg
Olms, 1962).

[84]Ibid., title page.

[85]Johann Nicolaus Forkel, <u>Allgemeine</u> <u>Geschichte</u> <u>der</u>
<u>Musik</u> (Leipzig: Schwickertschen Verlag, 1788, 1801).

[86]Ibid., pp. 1-68.

[87]Johann Nicolaus Forkel, <u>Ueber</u> <u>die</u> <u>Theorie</u> <u>der</u>
<u>Musik</u>, <u>insofern</u> <u>sie</u> <u>Liehabern</u> <u>und</u> <u>Kennern</u> nothwendig und
nützlich <u>ist</u> (Göttingen: Verlag der Wittwe Vandenhück,
1777).

[88]Ibid., pp. 6-7.

[89]Ibid., p. 4.

[90]Wolf Franck, "Musicology and its founder, J. N.
Forkel," <u>Musical</u> <u>Quarterly</u> 35 (1949):   593.

[91]Forkel, <u>Ueber</u> <u>die</u> <u>Theorie</u>, pp. 34-38. See
Appendix I in this study for a translation of Forkel's
outline.

[92]Franck, "Musicology," p. 593.

[93]François-Joseph Fétis, <u>Traité</u> <u>du</u> <u>contrepoint</u> <u>et</u>
<u>de</u> <u>la</u> <u>fugue</u> (Paris: Janet & Cotells, 1824).

[94]François-Joseph Fétis, <u>Traité</u> <u>de</u> <u>la</u> <u>theorie</u> <u>et</u> <u>de</u>
<u>la</u> <u>practique</u> <u>de</u> <u>l'harmonie</u> (Paris: M. Schlesinger,
1844).

[95]Ibid., p. ii.

[96]<Aristotle>, <u>Problemata</u>, XIX, 20, 36. In
paragraph 20 <Aristotle> questions: "Why is it that, if
one shifts the mese <tonic>, after tuning the <other>
strings, and then plays the instrument, it is not only
when the tune touches the sound of the mese that it is
unpleasant and seems out of tune, but also all the rest
of the melody?" It would be as if in a melody in C

major all the C's were to be played C#--the result
would be unpleasant and out of tune.

[97]François-Joseph Fétis, Biographie universelle des
Musiciens, 2nd ed. (Paris: Didot, 1873), p. iii.

[98]Ibid., p. viii.

[99]François-Joseph Fétis, Histoire Générale de la
Musique (Paris: Didot, 1869)

[100]Ibid., p. i.

[101]Ibid., p. 7.

[102]Fétis, Biographie Universelle, p. v.

[103]Alfred Einstein, Music in the Romantic Era (New
York: W. W. Norton, 1947), p. 47.

[104]Fétis, Histoire Générale, p. 7.

[105]Ibid., pp. 7-147.

[106]François-Joseph Fétis, Méthode des Méthodes de
chant (Paris: 1869).

[107]François-Joseph Fétis and Ignaz Moscheles,
Méthode des méthodes de piano (Paris: 1840).

[108]Moritz Hauptmann, The Nature of Harmony and
Meter, trans. W. E. Heathcote (London: Swan Sonenschein
& Co., 1888), p. xvii-xvii.

[109]Ibid., pp. xxxv-xxxvi.

[110]Ibid., p. xviii.

[111]Ibid., p. 5-6.

[112]Ibid., p. 9.

[113]Ibid., p. 10.

[114]Ibid., p. 11.

[115]Hugo Riemann, Hugo Riemann's Theory of Harmony and History of Music Theory, Book III, trans. and ed. William C. Mickelsen (Lincoln: University of Nebraska Press, 1977), p. 28.

[116]August Ambros, The Boundaries of Music and poetry, trans. J. H. Cornell (New York: G. Schirmer, 1893).

[117]Eduard Hanslick, Vom Musikalisch-schönen (Wiesbaden: Breitkopf & Härtel, 1978).

[118]Ibid., p. 2.

[119]Ambros, The Boundaries, p. v.

[120]Ibid.,p. xii.

[121]August Ambros, Geschichte der Musik (Leipzig: Leuckart, 1880).

[122]Ibid., vol. 1, p. 317f.

[123]Hermann von Helmholtz, The Mechanism of the Ossicles of the Ear and Membrana Tympani, trans. A. H. Buck and N. Smith (New York: William Wood & Co., 1873).

[124]Hermann von Helmholtz, On the Sensations of Tone as a Physiological Basis for the Theory of Music, trans. Alexander J. Ellis (New York: Dover Publications, Inc. 1954).

[125]Ibid., p. 1.

[126]Ibid., p. 2.

[127]Ibid., p. 4.

[128]Ibid., p. 371.

[129]Robert Eitner et al. Bibliographie der Musik-Sammelwerke des XVI. Jahrhunderts (Berlin, 1877; reprint ed., Hildesheim: Georg Olms, 1963).

[130]Ibid., p. v.

[131]Ibid., p. vi.

[132]Robert Eitner, Biographisch-Bibliographisches Quellenlexikon der Musiker und Musikgelehrten der christlichen Zeitrechnung bis zur Mitte der neunzehnten Jahrhunderts (Leipzig: Breitkopf & Härtel, 1900-1904).

[133]Ibid., p. 5.

[134]Ibid., p. 6.

[135]Hermann Kretzschmar, "Anregungen zur Förderung musikalischer Hermeneutik," Gesammelte Aufsätze aus den Jahrbüchern der Musikbibliothek Peters, vol. 2 (Leipzig: C. F. Peters, 1911), pp. 168-192.

[136]Ibid., p. 168.

[137]Hermann Kretzschmar, Führer durch den Konzertsaal (Leipzig: Breitkopf & Härtel, 1888-1890).

[138]Hermann Kretzschmar, Kleine Handbücher der Musikgeschichte nach Gattungen (Leipzig: Breitkopf & Härtel, 1919).

[139]Hugo Riemann, Grundris der Musikwissenschaft (Leipzig: Quelle & Meyer, 1928).

[140]Ibid., pp. 8-9.

[141]Hugo Riemann, Kleines Handbuch der Musikgeschichte mit Periodisierung nach Stil prinzipien und Formen, 5th ed. (Leipzig: Breitkopf & Härtel, 1932).

[142]Ibid., p. viii.

[143]Ibid., p. x-xii.

[144]Hugo Riemann, Studien zur Geschichte der Notenschrift (Leipzig: Breitkopf & Härtel, 1878).

[145]Ibid., pp. v and vii.

[146]Hugo Riemann, "The Nature of Harmony," in New Lessons in Harmony, by John Comfort Fillmore (Philadelphia: T. Preser, 1887), pp. 30-31.

[147]Hugo Riemann, Vereinfachte Harmonielehre, oder die Lehre von den Tonalen Funktionen der Akkorde (London: Augener and Co., 1893).

[148]Hugo Riemann, History of Music Theory (Books I and II), trans. R. H. Haggh (Lincoln: University of Nebraska Press, 1962). History of Music Theory, Book III, trans. W. C. Mickelsen (Lincoln: University of Nebraska Press, 1977), pp. 105-238.

[149]Hugo Riemann, Musik Lexikon, 11th ed. (Berlin: Max Hesses Verlag, 1929).

[150]Ibid., p. iv.

[151]Ibid., p. v.

[152]Guido Adler, "Umfang, Methode und Ziel der Musikwissenschaft," Vierteljahrsschrift für Musikwissenschaft, 1, (1885), 5-20. Translated by David R. Lively as "Scope, Method and Objective of Musicology."

[153]Friedrich Chrysander, ed., Jahrbücher für musikalische Wissenschaft (Leipzig: 1863, 1867; reprinted., Hildesheim: Georg Olms, 1966), p. 11.

[154]Adler, "Umfang, Methode...," p. 5.

[155]Ibid., pp. 6-7.

[156]Ibid., p. 8.

[157]Ibid., p. 15.

[158]Ibid.

[159]Ibid., p. 19.

[160]Ibid., p. 20.

[161]It might be objected, by the attentive reader,
that our 19th-century retrospective is excessively
Teutonic. That it is Teutonic goes without saying, but
not excessively so. For the most part, systematized
musicology is a German discovery. It is to these 19th-
century German writers that we must look for the formulations of the discipline that are still guiding it.

In order to understand anything,
one must understand everything;
but in order to say anything
one must leave out a great deal.
--Simone de Beauvoir

CHAPTER IV

A PHENOMENOLOGICAL CRITIQUE
OF MUSICOLOGICAL KNOWLEDGE

§ 10.   Sedimented concepts thematized

Now that a retrospective summary of the field of
musicology has been done, the subfields within
musicology have emerged and can be thematized and
described. From our historical study three basic
approaches to the phenomenon of music have manifested
themselves, music being the core of the musicological
field. These three approaches make up the ground of all
musicological study: they are the historical, practical
and systematic or speculative. Even attitudes toward
the core itself, music, undergo a change that is
parallel to the development of notation systems. The
two fundamental concepts of the originary phenomenon

"music" are that of the "unheard music" and the
"physically audible." Music in the first category is
humana, the harmony of body and soul. Also, in this
category is musica mundana, music of the spheres which
is best represented by number. Both of these ideas are
a reflection of the concept of harmonia, that which
works well together. St. Augustine <5.b.1>[1] defines
music as the science of mensurating or measuring well
(harmoniously), which is found in numerical relationships. These two aspects of music, even though we most
often think of music as an audible phenomenon, are still
sedimented in our attitudes toward music. The mathematical side of music is still relied upon for purposes
of analysis and compositional techniques in the 20th
century.[2]

Around this double musical concept there clusters
a number of areas of study that make up the body of the
science of musicology. Those that emerged in this study
are: the debate over methodology; the continuing bifurcation between historical (practical) and systematic
(theory) approaches; general music histories; performance
practice; bibliography and textual criticism; acoustics;
aesthetics and criticism; education in music; ethnomusicology; and music theory in general, which includes
compositional process, practical theory and speculative
theory. Parallel to these purely musicological studies,
the musicologist uses a variety of auxiliary sciences in
the study of music. These sciences include diplomatics,
archival research, biography, psychology, logic,
philosophy, etc.

The remainder of this chapter is devoted to
unpacking and spinning out these thematic musicological
regions. Let us turn, first, to the methodological
debate.

§ 11. The methodological debate

A method is a way of organizing, describing and
explaining experience, and is not to be confused with
the experience itself. For example, analyzing a J. S.
Bach chorale by using Roman numerals and chord inversion
figures is a method used to determine the nature of
chord progressions in particular chorales and, by
comparison, to make general statements about Bach's
harmonic language. The method, Roman numeral analysis,
is not to be confused with the experience of the chorale
itself.

Two fundamental methodological subregions emerge
from the retrospective: mathematical and scientific.
Mathematics is used by musicologists in one of two
ways, either in the service of a cosmology where
music and whole numbers are identical, or used to
express laws and rules drawn from musicological
experience. Pythagorean number theory is an example of
the first use of mathematics as method <5.a.1>. There
are three areas within the second use of mathematics.
They are most evident in acoustics, and applied and pure
music theory. The mathematico-physical acoustics of
Sauveur illustrates the use of mathematics to describe
acoustical phenomena <6.a>. The use of numbers in
figured bass to describe chord inversions will serve as

an example for applied music theory <6.d>. The
hypothetical scales and pitch relationships invented
by Ptolemy belong to the area of pure music theory
<5.a.5>. The subregions of mathematics may be outlined
as follows:

    I.   Cosmology

   II.   Experimental

        A.   Acoustics

        B.   Pure theory

        C.   Applied theory

The scientific methods are divided into two areas:
natural and human. These methods have been used by
musicologists to determine general musical characteristics either stylistically or theoretically. Stylistic
considerations or classification schemata belong to the
branch of musicology known as "historical"; purely
theoretical matters, both speculative and practical,
belong to the systematic side. The methods of the
natural sciences have been used, most notably, in
acoustics <6.a> and the physiology of hearing <8.d>.
Theories of music have been devised based on the
findings of physical acoustics, e.g., the nature of the
partial series as ground of triadic harmony. In order
to explain harmonic generation, Jean-Philippe Rameau
used the acoustics of Sauveur and the scientific method

devised by Descartes in his Discourse on Method <6.d>.
Some historical methods treat music as an isolated phenomenon to be studied as the natural sciences might
study physical phenomena <6.g>. On the other hand, the
human sciences (Geisteswissenschaften) offer the musicologist a scientific method that is humanistic, not
naturalistic, in approach. These methods, the human
studies, see music as a human creation, and, as such,
expressive of human psychical states. It is the aim of
these methods to interpret rather than explain human
phenomena. Thus, the exegetical tools of hermeneutics,
as used by Kretzschmar <8.f>, are deemed more appropriate for music as cultural-human phenomena than the
tools of the natural sciences.

The 20th century has continued this scientific
tradition and has emphasized that musicology itself is a
method among other methods. It is a matrix of specially
designed methods made for the study of all the parameters of the musical phenomenon. Within this methodological matrix two areas emerge: first, that the aim of
musicological method is the study of musical phenomena,
which are seen as existing in splendid isolation;
another, coming from the hermeneutical traditions of
Kretzschmar <8.f> and Riemann <8.g>, has emphasized man
as musician as the locus of study. This methodological
shift requires more from the historical methods traditionally used by musicology than they can deliver. A
whole host of sociological and anthropological methods
must be brought into play when one emphasizes the human
side of music.

Finally, it appears that while the study of music
was in the mode of speculation, as with the Ancients,
the major method used was mathematical, except, of
course, the observational methods of Aristotle and
Aristoxenus. However, as the ability to notate music
accurately grew and speculation was transformed into the
description of practice, the inductive methods came into
use. From the viewpoint of methodology, the rise of
accurate notation systems was crucial for the introduction of inductive or scientific methods. As long as
practicing musicians could not write down accurately all
the parameters of music, the theoretical or speculative
musician had nothing to describe scientifically. He was
forced to speculate mathematically. The original bifurcation of music into theory and practice was transmuted
into the systematic and historical study of music
because of the rise, during the Middle Ages, of systems
of notation. This brings us to our description and
clarification of the historical-systematic dyad.

§ 12.   The historical-systematic dyad

The ancients divided music into two area:
theoretical or speculative, and instruction or practice
(see Figs. 1 & 3). This is the ground out of which will
eventually grow the two modern divisions of historical
and systematic musicology. Because of time and the
fates, our knowledge of the musicology of the ancients
is one-sided--it is nearly all speculative. There are
momentary descriptions of musical practice in the
writings of some of our ancient authors, but these are

descriptions for educational or political purposes, not
historical ones. For example, in the Laws (700a-701a)
Plato describes music as it was in the past as a point
of comparison to the music of his own times. Also, in
the Republic (530d-531c) he describes the division
between theory and practice; but, again, it is for
educational purposes in answer to the question: "what
suitable studies have you to suggest?" <5.a.2>.
Aristotle, in the Politics (1341b), describes the
fantastic marvels of technique of some musicians, but
his purpose is also pedagogical not historical <5.a.3>.
Aristoxenus' description of some musical practices of
his day are as counterexamples to the way he thought
music ought to be <5.a.4>. These momentary descriptions
of musical practice eventually die out in the
overwhelming tide of speculation. It is not until St.
Odo of Cluny (10th century) that we get a musical
handbook and an attempt at a new notation <5.b.6>. It
is only when all the parameters of musical sound are
capable of being notated that musicologists will concern
themselves with this written record and there will
evolve out of the ancient division of "practice" what we
know as historical musicology. Speculative music theory
will remain on the level of speculation, but with the
advent of written music, theories will develop to
describe a wide variety of musical processes. This of
course would be impossible without notations that record
all the parameters of musical practice.

     Guido Adler, who set the tone of modern musicology
late in the 19th century, defines the historical
approach in the following terms:

The history of music is segmented according
to eras, greater and lesser, or according to
peoples, territories, provinces, cities, or
artistic schools; the summary is either temporal or local, or temporal and local. . . .
<T>he history of music will view artistic
creations as such, in their mutual concatenation and reciprocal influence, without
particular regard to the lives and effects of
individual artists who have taken part in
this continual development.[3]

The historical aspect of musicology will then focus on
the temporal and stylistic progress and change in the
historical flow of music. This focus will be on music
not the biography of the creator of the music, i.e.,
beware of the intentional fallacy. The history of
music, then, is a description of the varied ways in
which music has been and is practiced "in their mutual
concatenation and reciprocal influence."

To this historical project the 20th century has
adhered, in the main. Hans-Heinz Dräger has modified
the schema by adding such items as recording techniques,
the sociology of music and interdisciplinary studies.[4]
Charles Seeger, another 20th-century musicologist,
deprecates the traditional historical attitude qua
scientific. His claim is that music historians have
been doing historiography all this time. As he writes:

Surely, the historiography of music has its
aspects that can be approached by rigorously

> scientific methods; but there are many more
> that are matters of value judgment and still
> as many, or more, about which we can speak or
> write little and eventually nothing in terms
> of scientific method.[5]

He goes on to write that historians have "viewed their
job as an account of 'what' was" as a succession of
events. In the 19th century, under the pressure of
evolutionary theory the question was changed to "how did
what was come to be what was?" But they were still
insisting on a rigorously scientific history, i.e.,
historiography. What was produced was diachronic
history. Seeger's point is that genuine history must
also be synchronic: an unpacking of a complex of events
that may or may not have an evolutionary connection with
the past. Music history, then, would have to include
axiology and become cultural history.

According to Adler, the systematic side of
musicology "is founded on the historical past."
Systematic musicology is then subservient to historical
musicology. Nevertheless, it falls into three categories: speculative music theory; music aesthetics; and
music pedagogy.[6] Musicologists in the 20th century see
systematic musicology as the study of the nature and
properties of music as a cultural and physical phenomenon. Charles Seeger sees the whole of musicology in
terms of an interrelation of systematics and history.[7]
For example, any of Adler's subdivisions under the
historical guise could be dealt with theoretically,
i.e., synchronically. Notation can be viewed and

described in its historical aspects as an interpretation
of musical change; or a notation system can be isolated, studied and described empirically, abstracted
from the flux of musical events. Walter Wiora wants to
reopen, under the scrutiny of systematic musicology,
many of the old musical questions that seem to have been
lost in the 19th century's insistence on scientific
rigor, including such questions as: What is music?
What is the relationship of music to society? What role
does value theory play in the musical experience?[8]
These are all aesthetical questions and belong to that
area of our perception of music which Adler places in
the systematic camp <13.h>.

When J. N. Forkel <7> schematized the study of
music he ignored the ancient division of theory and
practice as historical and gave us a schema of purely
musical matters, feeling that a history could be written
of any of the divisions of study within that schema.
History, for Forkel, is the presupposition for there
being any music at all. When Guido Adler <9> gave his
final codification to musicology, final in the sense
that his codification is reflected in the way musicology
is divided in American universities today, he went back
to Aristides Quintilianus for the protoschema <5.a.6,
Fig. 3>. Adler ignores Forkel's codification but does
admit that systematic musicology is grounded in the
historical. The reason Adler bifurcated the study of
music in this ancient fashion was for the sake of
scientific objectivity. Music is "objectified" through
the printed record both in music theories and musical
scores. These objective records can be scrutinized in a
rigorous manner either historically or systematically.

What appears to have happened is that musicologists have
paid more attention to Adler's schema than to the explanation of that schema.   As a result, Adler's two divisions, in contemporary musicology, exist side by side in
isolation from each other.

    In conclusion: the modern division in the study of
music between historical and systematic has its roots in
the ancient division between practice and theory.
Modern historical musicology is the progeny of the
ancient division of practice.   Historical musicology, in
the Adlerian schema, is the study of musical practice.
But this study could only happen after an adequate
notation system evolved such that practicing musicians
could write down music.   This written musical record
could then be studied as any other written record.   The
ancient division of theory or speculative music is the
modern division of systematic musicology.   As the Middle
Ages progressed this division took on a dual nature:
the ancient concept of music as a reflection of cosmic
harmony was theologized, and the ever growing written
record was subjected to theoretical scrutiny and
analysis.   From the Middle Ages through the Renaissance
all the writers we studied in the retrospective were doing
music theory or systematic musicology with only passing
nods at music history.   These writers were engaged in
solving notation questions and in the codification, in a
theoretical fashion, of current musical practice often
trying to square that theory with what they thought
ancient theory might have been.   One might argue that
theory and practice for most of the Middle Ages and
Renaissance were essentially one.   Genuine music history
is a product of the Enlightenment when writers were

beginning to take an interest in the history of music qua
history. Even though this history is anecdotal in nature
it eventually developed into the cultural and scientific
histories of the 18th and 19th centuries.

Let us move to an analysis of the scope and limits
of the eleven regions within the field of musicology
that emerged from the retrospective. The following
section is organized according to Adler's plan: parts
a.-f. belong to his historical division and parts g.-k.
belong to that of systematic musicology.

§ 13. Analysis of the regions within musicology

a. Music history in general

Two fundamental styles of writing music history can
be gleaned from the survey: anecdotal and scientific.
The scientific historian's work can be further subdivided into two subregions: those using the methods
derived from the natural sciences; and those using the
methods of the human sciences or hermeneutics. These
two subregions are not mutually exclusive but reflect
an emphasis on either music as a natural phenomenon, or
music as a human phenomenon.

Anecdotal music history is narration of events and
answers Seeger's question "how was it?" Representative
anecdotal histories would be those of Athenaeus <5.a.6>
and Sir John Hawkins <6.g> whose approach is
encyclopaedic within the European tradition. Those

sections of all the works surveyed of Renaissance
writers who exhibit a glimmer of historical interest are
also anecdotal <5.d.1-4>. With most of these writers,
for example Pietro Aaron <5.d.2>, the recital of music's
past is not out of respect or a sense of historical duty
to the past, but to demonstrate to the present (16th
century) how much better music had become.

Those histories that are systematic and scientific
try to answer the question, also raised by Seeger, "how
did what was come to be what was?" This question is
answered in one of two ways. First, by seeing music
basically as an isolable phenomenon and subject to
objective scrutiny as any other isolable phenomenon such
as rocks or cows, etc. These historians generally see
music in evolutionary terms, as progress from one state
to another; this progress is capable of articulation by
determining cause and effect in the evolutionary cycles,
by classifying similarities and differences between
entities, and by devising explanatory hypotheses to
describe and account for these changes and categories.
Music histories that emphasize style belong to this
category. Nearly all the musicologists of the Age of
Reason <6> viewed music in evolutionary terms where each
succeeding era is seen as advancing beyond the capabilities of the previous age.

In the second (though not mutually exclusive)
approach, the musical exegete is going to emphasize
music as a cultural phenomenon, i.e., as a human enter-
prise. His interest is in interpretation within the
human-cultural context, not objective explication.

Music, for this ilk of historian, is going to be a
metaphor for the inner subjective human life as lived
individually and in a cultural context. His aim, then,
will be to unpack, through interpretation, the complex
fabric of human existence. J. N. Forkel is the first
music historian to take this humanistic approach,
believing that the historical progress of music is
deeply interwoven in the fabric of society <7>.
François Fétis' <8.a> philosophy of music history was
that of the inseparability of musical understanding from
the culture that generated the music. August Ambros
<8.c> explicitly rejected scientific methods as a means
to music history and adapted the Hegelian dialectic as
the means to understanding and explaining the changes in
cultural-music history.

The 20th century has produced music historians that
continue the traditions of the Romantic era. The
broader approach of the cultural historian was continued
by Wilibald Gurlitt (1889-1963), who believed that every
epoch has its own particular concept of the beautiful
and of meaning, which the historian can only articulate
in the frame of reference of that particular epoch.[9]
This hermeneutical approach is in direct line from
Hermann Kretzschmar's musical hermeneutics <8.f>.
Arnold Schering (1877-1941) is another historian using
the exegetical tools of hermeneutics in the search for
analogies between musical and literary symbols.[10] There
are other music historians in the 20th century who do
not explicitly follow the hermeneutical method, but
treat music in a more naturalistic way. Even though
these writers give passing nods to cultural influences,
music is treated as an isolated phenomenon to be

described in an objective scientific manner. Such
histories as those by Paul Henry Lang[11] and Donald Jay
Grout[12] fall into this category.

Another method of doing music history that came to
full bloom in the 20th century is the study of musical
style. Style is, generally, seen as a classification
schema. The style of a piece of music is the result of
methods used in treating all the musical parameters:
form, instrumentation, harmonic and rhythmic language,
etc. These characteristics fall into general categories
such as fugal style, chorale style, polyphonic style,
etc. Individual composers and schools of composition
have styles that can be described. Histories of musical
style are often in the subregion of the natural sciences as far as method of approach is concerned. The
History of Musical Style by Richard Crocker is an
example of a music history that belongs to the subregions of those works that use the methods derived from
the natural sciences.[13]

Music histories can be outlined in the following
way:

I.   Anecdotal

II.   Scientific

A.   Natural

B.   Humanistic

b. Lexicography

Lexicography is that region within the field of
musicology that offers musical data in dictionary form.
Five subregions within the region of lexicography
emerged in the retrospective. First, those dictionaries
that offer definitions of musical terms are represented
by the dictionary of Johannes Tinctoris <5.d.1> and
Johann Mattheson <6.c>. One of the most important lexi-
cographical projects of the 20th century belongs to this
subregion. It is the Handwörterbuch der musikalischen
Terminologie conceived by Wilibald Gurlitt and edited by
H. H. Eggebrecht.[14] The Handwörterbuch is an attempt
to trace the genealogy of musical terms much in the same
way as the Oxford English Dictionary fills such a
function for the English language.

Second, there are dictionaries that cover the
entire field of music. An example would be the
dictionary of Rousseau <6.e>. Two major 20th-century
music dictionaries that are comprehensive are The New
Grove Dictionary of Music and Musicians[15] and the German
lexicon Die Musik in Geschichte und Gegenwart.[16]

Third, there are those lexica that are biographical
in nature. An early example of a biographical
dictionary is Mattheson's Grundlage einer Ehrenforte
<6.c>. Nicolas Slonimsky's edition of Baker's Bio-
graphical Dictionary of Musicians (1978) also belongs to
this third subregion.[17]

Fourth, closely allied to the third subregion are
those bio-bibliographical dictionaries. Three examples

stand out from the retrospective: those of François
Fétis <8.a>, Robert Eitner <8.e>, and Hugo Riemann
<8.g>.

     Lastly, there are those dictionaries that cover
special musical topics. Two examples from the 20th
century belong in this category: Cobbett's Cyclopedic
Survey Chamber Music,[18] and Curt Sach's Real-Lexikon der
Musikinstrumente.[19]

                    c.   Notation

     Pitch, timbre, duration and intensity: these are
the parameters of music for which notations have been
developed. Ideas, concepts and audible phenomena need
to be recorded and preserved for future performance and
generations. Unless they are written down, they run
the risk of being either lost entirely or distorted.
Notation systems, historically, can be divided into five
main regions of study, which are not necessarily chronological: letter and cipher notation; neumatic notation;
mensural notation; common practice notation; and the
history of notation.

     Letter and cipher notations are those that use
letters of the alphabet or numbers to designate pitch.
The ancients used a letter notation that fell into
disuse in the West and was not reintroduced until the
10th century by Odo of Cluny <5.b.6> who thought that it
was Boëthian. This letter notation (solmezation) was
improved upon by Guido d'Arezzo <5.b.7>. Hermanus
Contractus <5.c.3> used a letter notation that was a

mixture of Greek and Latin characters plus symbols for indicating intervals. All of these letter notations, except possibly the ancient, are tied to a text for rhythm and meter. Jean-Jacques Rousseau introduced a cipher notation in the 18th century <6.e> which uses punctuation marks for rhythms.

Neumatic notations are those that use a modified form of Greek accent and breathing marks <5.b.5; 5.c.3>. The earliest form of these neumes do not indicate pitch but melodic contour.

Organization and division of the parameter of duration was first attempted in mensural notation. Thus the term "mensuration," the temporal relationship between pitches are now "measured" out. The basic method for distinguishing and organizing different durational values was through the shape of note-heads. The color of the notation was used to show changes in meter <5.c.3>. The three musicologists in our study who grappled with and partially solved the problems in notating duration are John of Garland <5.c.1>, Franco of Cologne <5.c.2> and Philippe de Vitry <5.c.3>.

Common practice notation is that notation that was exclusively used from around 1600 to the mid-20th century. The innovations that make up common practice notation belong to the Gothic and Renaissance periods. For example, the "dot" sometimes indicating temporal prolongation and mensuration signs (time signatures) belong to Philippe de Vitry <5.c.3>. In the 16th century, there was an attempt by Vicentino <5.d.4> to reintroduce the ancient enharmonic mode through a

modified form of common practice notation. These
notational innovations had to wait until the 20th
century when composers became interested in microtonal
music.

Finally, the history of notation is a product of
the 18th century with the work of J. N. Forkel <7>. In
the 19th century, the first full-blown history of notation by Hugo Riemann <8.g> appeared.

The 20th century has continued this historical
study of earlier notation systems and attempts to
decipher them and produce performance scores in modern
notation. Three such modern works on notation are:
Carl Parrish, The Notation of Mediaeval Music (1957)[20];
Willi Apel, Notation of Polyphonic Music, 900-1600
(1949)[21]; and Johannes Wolf, Geschichte der Mensural-
notation von 1250-1460 (1904).[22] With the proliferation
of musical styles and the advent of electronic and
computer music in the latter half of the 20th century,
music faces a crisis in notation similar to that of the
early Middle Ages. New sounds and new concepts of pitch
classes (microtonality) do not conform to common practice notation and new ways of writing down these sounds
must be discovered. There is little standardization in
20th-century notation and those composers using new
sounds often resort to inventing their own set of symbols for their particular musical style. In order to
read these notations the performer must consult a glossary of symbols that is often given with each piece of
music. There have been several attempts at codifying
this multitude of notations, most notably: J. Chailley,
Les notations musicales nouvelles (1950)[23]; Leon

Dallin's Techniques of Twentieth-Century Composition
(1974) has several sections on notation[24]; Reginald
Smith Brindle's The New Music (1975) has a glossary of
new notation symbols and discusses electronic music
notation[25]; Aspects of Twentieth-Century Music, edited
by E. Wittlich, has a long discussion of new notation
devices for rhythm[26]; and Music Notation in the
Twentieth Century by Kurt Stone is one of the most
comprehensive studies to date.[27]

    The study of notation is an area of musicology that
readily falls both in the traditional historical and
systematic regions. The mainline theorists such as
Guido d'Arezzo, Aaron, John of Garland belong,
notationally, in the systematic region because they were
working on practical theoretical problems in the clarification of notational problems. Those writers in the
20th century who attempt systematization of 20th-century
practice are working in the same area. However, such
writers as Forkel, Riemann, Parrish, Apel, and Wolf are
looking at notation from an historical perspective,
explaining past practice and producing transcription
techniques.

                    d.   Organology

    The study of musical instruments (mechanisms that
produce sounds used for musical purposes), or
organology, is divided into four regions: percussion
instruments; string instruments; wind instruments; and
electronic instruments. Technically these groups are
idiophones (struck, shaken, plucked and rubbed),

chordophones (plucked, struck or bowed), aereophones
(free vibrating reeds or enclosed columns of air), and
electrophones (sound electronically produced). Although
some early writers, Boëthius <5.b.3>, for example, considered the human voice an instrument (part of musica
instrumentalis) modern organologists do not so consider
it. Organology considers two aspects of instruments:
construction, which includes their acoustical characteristics; and how they are played, which includes their
use in society.

Three of these organological divisions are found in
the writings of Cassiodorus <5.b.4> where his "instruments of percussion" are idiophones, his "instruments of
tension" are chordophones and his "wind instruments" are
aereophones.

Isidore of Seville <5.b.5>, in his Etymologiae,
discusses a variety of musical instruments through the
etymologies of their names. He does this without any
general classification schema. From the next century we
get a small work on organ pipe scales and construction
from Odo of Cluny <5.b.6> called De fistulis.[28]

From the Renaissance we have two writers discussing
musical instruments. Johannes Tinctoris <5.d.1> writes
about the construction of wind and stringed instruments
in his De Inventione et usu Musicae (1480). Nicola
Vicentino <5.d.4> was interested in making a keyboard
instrument that would reproduce his music that reintro-
duces the enharmonic genre in the Greek style.

Marin Mersenne <6>, during the Age of Reason, left
descriptions and performance capabilities of both
Western and non-Western instruments in his Harmonicorum
instrumentorum. Johann Mattheson's major work, Der
Vollkomene Capellmeister (1739), contains a section of
the art of organ building which is one of the more
important treatments of the subject during the Baroque
period <6.c>. Two music historians, John Hawkins <6.g>
and François Fétis <8.a>, both treat musical instruments
in their respective histories. Fétis, being more systematic than Hawkins, is the fuller treatment. In the
Fétis history are many illustrations with the descriptions which, incidentally, cover a wide range of non-
European instruments.

Guido Adler <9> places the subject of musical
instruments in his historical division. He couples
organology with the rules of orchestration: "intimately
connected with the history of instrumentation is the
history of musical instruments, their construction and
utilization...."[29]

Organology did not come into its own until the 20th
century with the work of Curt Sachs and Erich von
Hornbostel. In 1913 Sachs published his Real-Lexikon
der Musikinstrumente which was an attempt to synthesize
knowledge about musical instruments on an international
basis.[30] The study of musical instruments is important
to ethnomusicologists in the discoveries of cross-
cultural ties deduced from instrument construction and
tunings. Organology is also important for the study of
performance practice. For example, the knowledge of
key-dip and key length in Baroque keyboard instruments

has a direct effect on fingering practices which is
related to articulation and phrasing.

e. Performance practice

Only as musicians became interested in the actual
performance of older music did they begin to ask questions abut the performance practices of the time when the
music was written. This desire is a product of the 19th
century.

Of the works that are concerned with performance
practice, the writing is generally descriptive of the
way musicians have performed. This descriptive mode can
be divided into two subdivisions: comparative and
practical. The comparative subclass would include
those writers from ancient times to the 19th century who
mainly compared the music practices of one epoch with
another or one culture with another. Such comparisons
are usually done for extra-musical reasons, for
educational-political purposes, as in Plato <5.a.2>; or
for demonstrating how one style of music is better than
another, as in Aristoxenus <5.a.4> or our Renaissance
musicologists <5.d>. The practical side deals with just
that--musical practice whose aim is accurate representa-
tions of music whose performance traditions are now
dead.

There is one major musical concept of the Age of
Reason that relates directly to performance, that is the
concept of the loci topici <6.c-d>. These compositional
devices, borrowed from rhetoric, were meant to convey a

variety of emotions, through performance, to the
listener. To the writers of that time knowledge of
these devices was necessary for musical communication
through compositional techniques. For the 20th century,
knowledge of the Doctrine of the Affections (<u>loci</u>
<u>topici</u>) is a tremendous help in understanding the musi-
cal language of the 17th and 18th centuries, and an aid
in the performance of that music.

The 19th century saw a tremendous rise in interest
in older music. This interest, unlike that of earlier
centuries, was directed toward performing this music.
François Fétis, in his piano method (1840), included
older keyboard music and made suggestions about
performance that were in line with the practice of
earlier centuries--all in the interest of a more
faithful rendition of older music <8.a>. Guido Adler
<9> calls performance practice "a knowledge of types of
artistic execution" and places it in the study of the
"historical succession of precepts."[31] As the art
progresses, Adler writes, performance techniques change,
as the vast changes in ornamentation bear witness.
Musicologists study and systematize these changes.

The 20th century has seen a proliferation of works
dealing with the performance of early music. The attitude espoused by these writers on performance is that
since music is an audible art our understanding of early
music might be enhanced if we could hear the music in as
close an approximation to the original sound as
possible. Several writers can be mentioned in this
regard: Arnold Dolmetsch's writings on the interpretation of 17th- and 18th-century music[32]; Adolf

Beyschlag's Die Ornamentik der Musik (1908)[33]; Robert
Donington's The Interpretation of Early Music (1974) is
one of the most comprehensive to date[34]; and Michael
Collin's The Performance of Coloration, Sesquialtera, and
Hemiolia (1450-1750) (1963).[35] It can be seen how the
area of performance practice overlaps that of organology,
notation and theory. Accurate organological descriptions
and reconstructions of instruments are vital for an
understanding of the performance practices of early music.
With notation it is even more evident because, in the case
of ornamentation, ornaments are often designated by their
own notational devices. Many of these signs are a mystery
because no description of how to perform them exists in
the contemporary literature; execution must then be
inferred.

        f.   Textual criticism and bibliography

     Paleography, diplomatics, editing, bibliography and
collation are some of the subjects that make up the
region of musicology known as textual criticism. The
whole process of producing a critical text also includes
the study of printing, paper making, illumination and
illustrations, the study of watermarks and inks which
aid in chronology decisions. There are three kinds of
editions possible that fall within the region of textual
criticism: Urtext, diplomatic and critical. An Urtext
edition is free from as many editorial additions as
possible, such as fingerings and phrase marks that are
not to be found in holographic sources. A diplomatic
edition was a hand-made facsimile of the original. If a

diplomatic edition is needed now it is usually produced
photographically or xerographically. A critical edition
is a transcription in modern notation, if necessary, which
records and attempts to account for all variants from
manuscript and printed sources and present an edition as
close as possible to the "original."

This whole procedure has produced, in critical
editions, the collected works of a whole host of
composers and musicologists. There are also any number
of series devoted to the national music of individual
countries; these are called monumental series. This
production of collected works started in 1850 with the
foundation of the Bach Gesellschaft, which did not complete the edition of J. S. Bach's works until the end of
the century. The source book for all such collected
works and music monuments is Anna Harriet Heyer's
Historical Sets, Collected Editions, and Monuments of
Music (1980).[36]

Bibliography, an area closely allied to that of
textual criticism, is the assemblage, in chronological,
alphabetical or subject order, of publications on a
particular subject. These entries may contain just
publication data or be annotated (see Forkel <7>), or
give the location of copies (see Eitner <8.e>). In the
case of a bio-bibliography, the bibliography is in a
short biographical sketch of the individual in question
(see Fétis <8.a>).

The first music bibliography was published in
1792 by J. N. Forkel <7>. Forkel's scholarship and
attention to detail set the tone for all future music

bibliographies. Robert Eitner was the bibliographer of
the Romantic Age <8.a>. Eitner's goals and intentions,
to bring together in bibliographical volumes all the
available music source material for the use of musicologists, have been continued into the 20th century by the
International Musicological Society and the International
Association of Music Libraries in its publication International Inventory of Musical Sources (RISM). Another
branch of bibliography that is important are thematic
indexes of composers' works that contain bibliographic
histories of works and the literature on works. Notable
catalogues are those of Ludwig von Köchel for Mozart,
Wolfgang Schmieder for J. S. Bach, and Josef Rufer for
Schoenberg.

Bibliography, critical editions of music and
theoretical works are all indispensable tools for
musicologists. Research in any of these musicological
regions would be impossible without these assemblages of
musical materials. Even though Guido Adler placed these
two regions in his "auxiliary" category (see Appendix II),
they deserve a place of much more importance, as they are
the mainstay of musicological research. Textual
criticism, it must be noted, is one of the avenues that
performing musicians have to the processes of musicological research. Without the work of musicologists
there would be no Urtext or critical editions from
which to perform. Indeed, for much music from the past
there would be no readily available scores at all,
Urtext or otherwise.

g. Acoustics

Acoustics is the study of the physical properties of sound
and is divided into three areas: mathematical, physical,
and physiological. Mathematical acoustics is the oldest
of them and is still used as a means of expressing
acoustical laws. It originally was used to show the
relationship between intervals and as a description of the
difference between consonance and dissonance. Physical
acoustics is the study of the empirical characteristics of
sound itself such as the frequency of vibrations,
sympathetic vibrations, etc. Physiological acoustics
studies the way in which sound is transmitted by the ear
and the relationship of those findings to the perception
of difference in sound both as to pitch and quality.

An ancillary region within acoustics that occupied
the Renaissance was tuning and temperament. Renaissance
musicologists like Pietro Aaron <5.d.2> grappled with
problems inherent in Pythagorean tuning. Aaron proposed
a new tuning system called mean tone that would allow an
expanded gamut that would stay in tune with itself. The
problem is this. In the Pythagorean system the intervals are pure, i.e., acoustically correct, for a very
short range. As the range of pitches is increased or
chromatic alternations are added these additional tones
are inadequate, that is, out of tune. A pure or
Pythagorean fifth can produce a range of five or six
fifths, c, g, a, e, b. If one were to add successive
fifths that are chromatic, f, c, g, d, they cannot be
added to the pure fifths and be satisfactory. Thus,
methods are devised that spread this inaccuracy over all
the notes. Aaron's suggestion is slightly to flatten

the fifth c̲, g̲, to reconcile the Pythagorean comma.
Other Renaissance writers considered other acoustical
questions, e.g., the overtone series. Galileo <5.d>
gives one of the first explanations of the partial
series in his dialogue on the new sciences.

The writers of the Enlightenment finally formalized
many acoustical rules and devised more tuning systems as
music became more and more chromatic and composers started
using more and more of the available major and minor
modes. Marin Mersenne <6> worked a great deal with pitch
determination and string length. His research culminates
in a complete mathematization of pitch determination
without hearing the string at all. Descartes <6>
accomplished much the same acoustical work as his friend
Mersenne through scientific descriptions of the overtone
series and sympathetic vibrations.

Joseph Sauveur <6.a> wrote on all aspects of
acoustics, which he called the science of sound in
general. His work spanned the measuring of intervals
and pitches through their frequencies, the division of
the octave into enough parts so as to completely elimi-
nate any out-of-tuneness, and a complete study of the
harmonic series. Sauveur's work is independent of music
and he compares its relationship to music as the same
between optics and things seen. It was up to the music
theorist Jean-Philippe Rameau <6.d> to combine the use
of mathematics and acoustics to formulate a new music
theory. What Rameau puts together are the mathematical
(numerical relationships of intervals) and acoustical
(harmonic series) properties of sound to found his
harmonic theory.

In the 19th century Moritz Hauptmann went against
the mathematico-acoustical tradition as a basis for
harmonic theory because of the discrepancies in the
harmonic series, tuning systems and musical notation.
Hermann von Helmholtz, also in the 19th century, was the
founder of physiological acoustics. His interest was in
determining how the ear works. There are mathematical
applications in his physiology, as in any physical science, but his major interest was the transmission of sound
by the bones of the ear. From these studies he postulated
a music theory based on the physical properties of sound
coupled with the physiological transmission of that sound
to the brain.

Acoustics has applications in other regions within
musicology. We have seen how the discovery and description of the harmonic series influenced the formulations
of practical music theory along naturalistic lines.
Acoustics is also necessary in the region of organology.
Instrument building relies heavily on the acoustical
properties of the materials out of which the instruments
are made. These acoustical properties affect not only the
tuning capabilities of instruments, but also their timbre.

h.   Aesthetics

Aesthetic theories are divided into three major
types: mimetic, formalistic, and existential. The
mimetic or representational theory is further subdivided
into two fundamental types: those that take the point
of mimesis as fidelity to natural objects and those
that take the point of mimesis as fidelity to human

affections. The formalists feel that artistic worth must
be grounded on internal formal principles derived from
the art works themselves, not the degree of imitation
achieved by the artist and his work. An existential
theory combines all the aspects of our musical perceptions
by treating them as synaesthetic experiences.

Let us go to the ancients and follow through each
major period to summarize the aesthetic thinking of each
epoch. From Plato <5.a.2> through most of the 19th
century, theories devised to account for our perception
of objects about which we make axiological statements
can be summed up in one word: mimetic. The level of
imitation was seen as either of Nature or the laws
governing the universe. Thus the Pythagorean relationship
between number and musical sound was considered to be a
direct mimetic reflection of cosmic order. As human
beings we are miniature reflections of that cosmic order,
just as music is a reflection of cosmic law. If music
becomes out of tune with this law, it can create a
disharmonious human being. Music, then, has a direct
influence on the ethos of being human.

This theory of mimesis held for nearly all the
Medieval writers on music who emphasized the mathematical side of music which was then seen as a reflection of God's harmonic laws that govern the universe.
John Scotus Eriugena <5.b> believed that the locus of
beauty is in the numerical intervals of sounds which are
perceived by the soul, not by the ear. This numerical
ratio or proportion is what counts as beauty to most
Medieval thinkers. There were a few Medieval musicologists who were more practical in nature and seemed to

shy away from a cosmological aesthetics. John of
Garland <5.c.1> is one of these writers, as his definition of music from his De Musica Plana demonstrates:
"music is knowledge of accurate singing, or an easy
means of achieving perfection in singing."

   For our Renaissance writers on music the
reintroduction of Greek studies merely reinforced the
idea of music as mathematics. Composers copy the
harmonious relationships that exist on a cosmic level,
these writers held. They also continued the ancient
belief in the ethical effects of music. There is,
however, the beginnings of a shift in emphasis from God
and the universe to Man and the universe. Johannes
Tinctoris <5.d.1> still thinks of music in its cosmic
aspect, but adds a humanistic idea that it must also be
pleasing to people. This addition of pleasure can only be
based on current musical practice and the fact that the
human agent, as composer and performer, is becoming
increasingly important. Music is slowly becoming an art
of human proportions, not an art that reflects the work of
the God-mathematician. When we come to the writings of
Zarlino <5.d.4> at the end of the Renaissance we find the
art of composition a human product not an inspiration.
Zarlino relies on experience as the starting point in
aesthetics and criticism. It is only after experience
that reason can do its critical work. As he writes of the
music critic in his Istitutioni harmoniche (1571), that
person must be conversant in the theoretical as well as
the practical side of music. The music critic must not
only be able to understand the theory of music, he must
also be able to write music. Zarlino continues that
tradition of the ethical import of music. He sees the aim

of music to "guide the passions and lead the soul to virtue."[37]

The Age of Reason added one more facet to this mimetic theory: the Doctrine of the Affections (loci topici) <6.c-d>. The Doctrine of the Affections is mimetic in the sense that the level of mimesis or representation is no longer fidelity to Nature, but a representation or expression of human emotions and feelings. The worth of music is now the degree of fidelity of expression to the emotions, not Nature. Rousseau <6.e> had a different aesthetic battle to fight. It was, however, the complexity of music at that time that led him to advocate a return to the Greek ideals of clarity and simplicity. Melodies that are easy to sing and remember, simple harmonies and the absolute fusion of text and music, these are at the bottom of Rousseau's aesthetics, and any composer who did not conform felt the barb of his critical tongue.

There was a major shift in the 19th century away from these mimetic theories and a move to what has been termed "formalism." Eduard Hanslick's little volume Vom musikalisch-schönen (1854) is an attempt to abandon this reliance on emotions and feelings as a critical and explanatory tool in music aesthetics and criticism <8.c>. He desires an objective aesthetics, i.e., one based on the methods of the natural sciences.

Guido Adler <9> at the end of the 19th century outlines an extensive project for the aesthetics of music.[38] In the outline (see Appendix II) he writes that aesthetics is the "comparison and evaluation of the

percepts and their relation to the apperceiving subject
for the purpose of establishing the criteria of the
musically beautiful."

    Susanne K. Langer, in the 20th century, has
continued Hanslick's line of formalistic thought. For
Langer, music criticism is not concerned with the
explication of a "text" on its own terms and merits. She
includes in this extra-artistic category all biography and
psychology. This interpretive project has much in common
with the New Criticism in literature. To paraphrase these
schools of thought, the watchword is: "to the text
itself!"

    Another aesthetic and critical movement in the 20th
century is that of existential criticism. Existentialists
point out that our aesthetic experiences, indeed all
experience, is actually synaesthetic. Experiences are not
just visual, not just audible, they are a mixture of all
the senses, although our mental focus or attention may
shift from one to the other. Aesthetic theory must
account for this blending of experiences, not just isolate
one as if it were all-inclusive. In the musical
experience it is not just sound we experience, it is also
visual. Even though the visual aspects might be
background they are still there and affect the experience.
There are musical experiences that are an equal blend of
the visual and audible: opera for example. Some modern
composers have also brought other senses into play, for
example by using odors during performances.
Existentialists claim that were our ordinary experiences
NOT synaesthetic, art forms that combine the senses into
one sensorium would not have developed.

i. Education in music

"Pedagogy," "didactics," "paideutics": all of
these are closely related terms for education in music.
This region of musicology is divided into two broad
areas: music used as an educational tool for extra-
musical purposes, and the teaching of music itself.

In Book X of the Republic, Plato <5.a.2> rebukes
the poets (including Homer) for teaching the people
falsehoods about the gods and matters of which they, the
poets, have only second-hand knowledge. Plato insists
that poetry and music be brought under the tight control
of the state. Poetry, for Plato, was the primary teaching
medium of Hellas. On the other hand, Aristotle <5.a.3>
writes in the Politics (1341b) that everyone should
have some musical education, but not to the point of
making professionals out of them. Music should be used
for personal improvement not vulgar display.

At the beginning of the Middle Ages, Boëthius
<5.b.3> gave to the educational system the divisions of
the quadrivium and the trivium. Odo of Cluny and Guido
d'Arezzo <5.b.6-7> wrote the first music handbooks
designed to teach singing to boys and simple persons.
Heinrich Glarean, in the Renaissance, wrote an isagoge
which is a complete music handbook for school use
<5.d.3>. It is an introduction to all aspects of music,
both theoretical and practical. In this same work
Glarean gives some advice to teachers to the effect that
if you do not know something, say so; do not try to
disseminate false knowledge because of false pride.

Friedrich Marpurg, in the 18th century, wrote
didactic works on keyboard performance, thorough-bass
and composition <6.f>. His keyboard book of 1762 covers
an introduction to the keyboard itself, elementary harmony
and how to read music, and a section on the performance
practice of his time. The first part ends with a section
on fingering. The second part deals with accompaniment
and thorough-bass realization.

In the 19th century François Fétis <8.a>
contributed two works on teaching. There is a voice and
a piano method. These two works are also an inventory
of vocal and piano methods. Hermann Kretzschmar <8.f>
applied his method of musical hermeneutics to the teaching
of music. He wanted to effect a more general education of
the concert-going public, and not just have music
education reside in conservatories and universities.

Guido Adler <9> places music pedagogy and didactics
third in line under systematic musicology and divides it
into six parts (see Appendix II). Not only does he
include in this schema education in music, but also all
the sections of music theory and composition. His
rationale is "if the rules are established in abstracto
and founded scientifically, they are then classified and
summarized with regard to educational purposes."39
Once, for example, the theory of counterpoint has been
done, then one can use that theory for educational
purposes. An example might be Fux's Gradus ad
Parnassum, which is both a compendium of Renaissance
modal counterpoint and a textbook from which students
are taught contrapuntal techniques of the late Renaissance.

Music education in the 20th century has centered largely around teaching individuals to teach, and devising a plethora of methods pursuant to that end. One must also include in these methodologies a host of methods for teaching people to play musical instruments, and all aspects of music theory. In the United States, music education in the public schools is generally performance-oriented. The presence of performing groups in public schools soon gave rise to the need for classroom instruction in applied music.

Two examples of 20th-century methods used in music education are those by Zoltan Kodaly (1882-1967) and Carl Orff (1895-1982). Fundamental to Kodaly's method is his belief that everyone should have some musical skills. The younger we start children the faster they will learn. His method is based on singing as the musical instrument with which we are all born. He uses childhood chants, nursery rhymes, etc., as a starting point. There is then a gradual accumulation of skills and literature. The components of the system are a set of duration symbols for rhythm, use of the movable <u>do</u> system in teaching melodies, and a series of hand signs, reminiscent of Guido's hand, to indicate pitch and pitch relationships. [40]

Carl Orff's <u>Schulwerk</u> contains the outlines of his method. [41] This includes the teaching of pentatonic scales and basic rhythm patterns. He uses musical instruments as the teaching modes, along with singing. This whole method is based on an historical approach, i.e., children learn music the way in which music developed.

j. Ethnomusicology

Guido Adler <9> calls ethnomusicology "musicology"
and defines it as an "examination and comparison for
ethnographic purposes."[42] He also calls this region
"comparative musicology" and writes that it is its task
to compare the musical products of "various peoples,
countries, and territories" according to their separate
natures.[43]

Jean-Jacques Rousseau <6.e> is the first of our
musicologists to write about non-European music. His
dictionary of 1765 contains descriptive articles about
oriental music and examples of Chinese, Canadian Indian,
Swiss and Persian music. Sir John Hawkins <6.g>, in his
music history (1776), acknowledges that other peoples
have music but that he cannot treat of them because
these musics are unscientific and he is not equipped to
delve into their aesthetic natures, if any.

The first full treatment of non-European music
comes from the pen of François Fétis <8.a>. His
Histoire générale de la Musique (1869) is an approach
to music that includes anthropology and ethnology, as he
believes that such studies are necessary to an adequate
understanding of music as a human endeavor. The history
of music is inseparable from the understanding of the
special qualities of the people that cultivate the art.
Such an attitude comes from a belief that music changes,
it does not progress, any question of a constant movement to perfection is out of place. With this
background, Fétis opens his music history with a long
study of non-European music. All aspects of musicology

proper, e.g., organology, music theory, etc., are
brought to bear on his discussions of non-Western music.

In the 20th century, Jaap Kunst first applied the
name "ethnomusicology" to what Guido Adler called comparative musicology.[44] Ethnomusicology is thus conceived as a combination of musicology and cultural
anthropology. Ethnomusicology concerns itself with
three types of music: the music of non-literate
societies, Asian and north African high cultures, and folk
music. Such societies as the American Indians, Black
Africans, and Australian aborigines are considered non-
literate or "pre-literate" cultures. The music of most
Asian cultures, Iran and Arabic-speaking societies is
distinguished from pre-literate societies by a complex
style, the presence of professional musicians, a theory of
music and a system of notation. Folk music is that music
which exists embedded in a high culture that is passed on
in oral tradition.[45] The emphasis in ethnomusicology
is on non-Western and folk music. As far as the music
itself is concerned:

> most ethnomusicologists agree that the
> structure of music and its cultural context
> are equally to be studied, and that both must
> be known in order for an investigation to be
> really adequate.[46]

Within this study there are six major areas of
attention: 1) instruments, or organology, 2) song
texts, 3) native typology and music classification,
4) the rôle and status of musicians within a given
culture, 5) the function of music in relation to other

aspects of the culture, and 6) music seen as a creative
activity. All ethnomusicologists agree on the utmost
importance of field work in order to come to terms with
these areas mentioned above. Mantle Hood, in his book
on ethnomusicology, warns that the ethnomusicologist runs
the risk of a too broad approach in attempting an all-
encompassing comparative approach.[47] There is one
other area of study for ethnomusicologists that must be
mentioned before we move on, and that is one which entails
the study of the "shaping of a musical culture in which
Western and native elements are combined."[48] The
Orient is an area where this approach is fruitful.

One further point: ethnomusicologists are going to
be more concerned with method than most musicologists.
This is so because they have to deal with alien cultures
and will need to bring into play the methods, concepts,
and ideas borrowed from anthropology, archaeology and
the social sciences in order to do their work. Finally,
an item that all anthropologists and ethnomusicologists
must face is the question of how deeply enmeshed in an
alien society must one become before one's work is
credible. This is, basically, a question of cultural
objectivity. The point is raised that becoming too
intimate in an alien culture will impair the anthropolo-
gist's ability to describe objectively that particular
society. However, one must become engaged to some
degree in order to know what to describe and explain in
the complex relationships that characterize all
cultures. As far as the ethnomusicologist is concerned,
knowledge of that culture's language, some proficiency
on their musical instruments, notations (if any) and
religious and societal connections with that music would

seem to be mandatory. As a matter of fact, these are the same basic items one would expect a musicologist studying Western music to know.

k. Music theory

Music theory combines both normative and descriptive traits. As normative, music theory formulates the rules and norms that govern the art of music. Once these rules are systematized, they can then be used for purposes of description and analysis. Within this region of musicology, three subregions emerge from our analysis. They are those works that deal with the compositional process, works that are of a practical bent, i.e., those works that devise rules and descriptive procedures drawn from musical practices, and those theoretical works that are in the subregion of speculative music theory. This last category covers nearly all music theory written through the 10th and 11th centuries, that is until the advent of advanced notational systems. These speculative theories usually include the use of mathematics as the descriptive tool.

These subregions of music theory share some characteristics. For example, those works that deal with the compositional process can also belong in the practical subregion. Once a compositional style has been developed and described, it can then be used to describe and analyze other music. On the other hand, theory books that are normative in nature, those dealing with harmonic and contrapuntal practice and analysis, can be used as rule books for composition. Fux's counterpoint book, which is

normative, i.e., gives all the rules for writing good
counterpoint, can be used as a compositional guide for
writing works in that genre.

1. Compositional processes

Several of our musicologists have contributed to
this subregion. The first to write about a specific
compositional process is Guido d'Arezzo in his Micrologus
<5.b.7>. His is a method of composing chant lines by
matching the vowels in a predetermined text to the letter
names of the pitches in the gamut. Johannes Tinctoris in
his Contrapuncti (1477) devotes a whole section to the art
of improvisation <5.d.1>. Pietro Aaron <5.d.2>, in 1516,
offers some suggestions to composers that have been
followed to this day: a harmonic (vertical) not
contrapuntal (horizontal) technique. This change is
indicative of a gradual shift from contrapuntal to
harmonic thought in compositional processes. Aaron also
suggests that composers desist from the practice of musica
ficta--from now on write in all accidentals. At the end
of the Renaissance, Zarlino was writing music theory from
the standpoint of a practicing composer <5.d.4>. Being
able to compose music is fundamental, writes Zarlino, to
anyone who proposes to write about music. His Istitutioni
(1558) is both normative and descriptive of the
compositional practices of the late Renaissance.

Johann Mattheson and Jean-Philippe Rameau, during
the Enlightenment, write about the loci topici and their
use in musical composition to arouse certain passions in
the listener <6.c-d>.

There have been many 20th-century composers who
have written on the compositional process. We will
consider four of them as representative: Arnold
Schoenberg (1874-1951), Paul Hindemith (1895-1963),
Olivier Messiaen (1908-), and Iannis Xenakis (1922-).

Schoenberg is best known for his discovery of the
method of composition called "12 tone", in which the
feeling of tonality is denied by equalizing the importance
(harmonically) of all the pitches of the chromatic scale.
This system is the logical conclusion to the high degree
of chromaticism of late-19th-century music. Although
Schoenberg wrote little about this method and never taught
it officially, he did write a composition book for tonal
music: Fundamentals of Musical Composition (1937-1948).[49]
This work, as nearly all of Schoenberg's didactic works,
aims at teaching the musical amateur through an analysis
of works of master composers, e.g., Beethoven, and writing
music in all forms based on that analysis. Schoenberg
felt most strongly, that before an individual could launch
into some new method of composition he needs to be well
grounded in the music of the past. For Schoenberg, the
foundation of all harmonic theory and thought is the
harmonic series. This includes the 12-tone method; all of
the pitches of the chromatic scale are present in the
partial series.

Hindemith also believes that the harmonic series is
the natural ground for there being any music, but would
not go so far as to deny the naturalness of tonality.
He did believe, and practice, that chords do not, of
necessity, have to be built up of thirds; fourths might
do just as well.[50]

Messiaen, in his The Technique of My Musical
Language, expounds new methods of composition dealing
mainly with pitch organization and rhythm concepts.[51]
Messiaen has devised a series of "modes" or arrangements
of pitches of the chromatic scale from which he draws
his melodic and harmonic language. Messiaen's rhythmic
concept is essentially ametrical in that the music is
unmeasured but the notations are exact. He chooses a
short rhythmic value as a constant upon which he can
freely multiply rhythms.

Finally, Xenakis in his Formalized Music: Thought
and Mathematics in Composition (1971) takes the reader
into the realm of almost complete abstraction of the
compositional process. There are three classes of
compositional techniques used by Xenakis: stochastic,
which uses the calculus and theory of probability;
strategic, based on the theory of games; and symbolic,
based on mathematical logic and set theory.[52]

All of these compositional methods are practical in
nature--one can learn to compose music or use certain
compositional devices in composition. All of them are
grounded in natural (harmonic series) law, except that
of Xenakis which is based completely on mathematical
processes.

2. Practical

There emerges from the study four subregions
of practical music theory: mathematical-acoustics;
humanistic-cultural; musical dialectics; and

physiological acoustics. Mathematical-acoustics is
represented by the work of Sauveur <6.a> in acoustics, and
Rameau <6.d>, who founded his harmonic theory on Sauveur's
mathematical acoustics, which is an exposition of the
heard partials as expressed mathematically. The second
group, humanist-cultural, is represented by the work of
Fétis <8.a>. Music for Fétis is a creation of human
culture and must be analyzed in that frame of reference.
Musical dialectics is the work of Moritz Hauptmann <8.b>,
who felt that the discrepancies between harmonic practice
and the partial series nullified its use as a natural
ground for harmonic language. He substituted as an
explanation of this language an abridged form of Hegel's
dialectics. Lastly, physiological acoustics as a basis
for harmonic theory is Hermann von Helmholtz's idea <8.d>.
Helmholtz, through the study of the transmission of sound
by the inner ear and the power of immediate sound
sensation, builds a harmonic theory to account for tonal
practice.

There are many 20th-century writers who have
written harmony books based on common practice music.
Those by Arnold Schoenberg, Walter Piston and Robert
Ottman are representative. All of these writers, either
implicitly or explicitly, base their theories on mathematics and physiological or physical acoustics.

Heinrich Schenker (1868-1935) devised an analytical
method that is original. Neue musikalische Theorien und
Phantasien (1906-1935) is a new method of looking at and
analyzing the musical logic of tonal music.[53]
Schenker's system is grounded in musical practice,
actual music, and is meant for the use of performers,

not theoreticians. His purpose is to develop a method
that will allow the musician to understand the basic
structure of a piece of music through the logic of its
form. For Schenker, form and key-area are interdepen-
dent: tonality creates form. To understand this
relationship Schenker "de-composed" the music down to its
most elemental formal characteristics, both melodic and
harmonic.

Another development in the 20th century was an
analytical tool for handling non-common practice music,
e.g., atonality, which does not submit to common practice analytical techniques. The work of Alan Forte, The
Structure of Atonal Music (1973), is a work that evolves
techniques for analyzing atonal music (not 12-tone).[54]
Basically, this is an application of mathematical and
set theory to atonal music. Collections of pitches are
reduced to sets and their behavior as set complexes can
be observed by the methods devised by Forte. These 20th-
century analytical developments by Schenker and Forte
can be placed in our humanistic-cultural subregion, as
they are based completely on already composed music and
not on acoustics or a mathematical model.

3. Speculative

Speculative music theory held sway from Pythagoras
through the late Middle Ages. The only exceptions are
<Aristotle's> Problemata and Aristoxenus' Harmonics
which are a description of musical practice de-mathema-
tized, especially in the case of Aristoxenus <5.a.3-4>.
For Aristotle, it is not mathematics as such that is

objected to, but number-magic. This whole subregion of
speculative theory was music theory for the sake of some
extra-musical purpose, usually to show a cosmological
connection of the harmonious relationships that exist in
number. It could be used to show, as metaphor, the
relationship between body and soul. In the Middle Ages
music theory was an explanation of the harmonious nature
of the relationship between God, Man, and the Universe.
It is with the rise of the ability to write down, with any
accuracy, music as practiced that theorists have turned to
that written record and attempted descriptive explanations
of it. The force of the speculative tradition was so
strong that throughout the Renaissance and into the Age of
Reason this body of speculative theory was the model for
practical music theory. Music was still answering to
mathematics. Speculative music theory and its number-
magic eventually died out with the advent of humanism in
the Renaissance and the use of scientific methods in the
Enlightenment.

§ 14. Auxiliary sciences

Auxiliary sciences are those areas of study which
have a life of their own completely separate from musicology's project, but which nevertheless are sometimes
used by musicologists as aids in their work. Many of
these have been mentioned in the retrospective. All of
these sciences concomitant to writing general history
are such auxiliary sciences: paleography, the study of
writings; chronology aided by the study of paper making
and water marks; diplomatics, the use of archives as a
source. Linguistics can be used in the study of texts

used in musical settings. Rousseau's belief that French
cannot be set to music is a result of his linguistic
musings. Biography and psychology are also used in
musicological research. Adler notes, however, that
"biography has forced its way into the foreground
disproportionately, has even comported itself as
musicology's kat' exochen," i.e., chief man.[55] The
problem that Adler is hinting at is that excessive
reliance on biographical or psychological data, derived
from biography, may lead the musicologists to commit the
intentional fallacy. When this happens, the critical
evaluation and analysis of musical works stems from
psychological data and not musical data. Dika Newlin has
written on this problem in her article "The 'Mahler's
Brother Syndrome': Necropsychiatry and the Artist."[56]
The article is a plea for musical understanding first and
foremost in musical terms.

When data acquired from extra-musical disciplines
and sources that are used for the analysis of music
become more important and influential than the music
itself, we term them "musicologisms."

§ 15.   Conclusions and projections

In drawing this project to a close I would like to
do two things as a conclusion: show how the phenomenological method was used in doing the critique; and
suggest a different schema for the discipline of musicology based on the critique.

Phenomenology is a method used to describe regions of consciousness. It is an ephectic method in that it consciously brackets and suspends judgments about those regions that are not germane to the particular study under way. The region of consciousness chosen for this study is musicology. Musicology is a region of consciousness because it is a construct of human ratiocination. Musicology consists in thought about the human experience of music, but thought of a systematic or scientific nature. From this fundamental definition it is obvious that the major area to be put out of use, bracketed, is music itself. We are projecting a critique about the systematic thought about music, not music itself. The second area to be bracketed is musicology itself. This study is not musicology nor is it a musicological work, it is metamusicology. It is a phenomenological analysis of the field of musicology.

The method used for starting such a phenomenological project is historical, as outlined by Edmund Husserl in his Crisis of European Sciences. Musicology is a project that is under way, it has a history. One way of approaching the question of a critique is through a retrospective: disclose, historically, the writings of musicologists. From this disclosure the various regions that musicologists have written about will emerge. Once the retrospective is done, these regions can be pulled together and described as to similarities and differences. Since this has been done, to a certain extent, by J. N. Forkel and Guido Adler, their schemata can be taken as staring points for the descriptive and critical sections. Each region is then described as to its essential meanings and any similarities with other regions noted.

One aspect of these regions that is at variance with
Adler's schema was clarified through the technique of
free imaginative variation. It was noticed that these
regions had histories written of them, indeed it can be
imagined that a history could be written of all of them
by varying the intentional focus on that region. For
example, organology, depending upon focus, can be seen
as either part of acoustics or the history of musical
instruments. Notation, also, is both part of compositional processes and practical music theory, and the
history of notation can be written, all depending upon
the intentional focus needed or desired.

As far as the domain of future-applied musicology
is concerned, three areas need to be discussed: methodology, musicologisms and the historical-systematic division in 20th-century musicology.

a. Methodology

The general focus of the methodology of musicology
should be that of the human studies (Geisteswissenschaften). Both musicology and the music it studies are
human constructs. Music is an art, a techne, a thing
made by humans manipulating the medium of sound much in
the same way a sculptor manipulates the medium of stone,
etc. The study of music would be best served if it
concentrated on the human, therefore cultural, context
of music's genesis and constitution. While the methods of
the natural sciences prove useful in the study of sound as
sound, the application of these methods to all things
musical has a tendency to ignore the human factor in music

and treat the phenomenon as if it existed in splendid
isolation. Pure description of musical phenomena, i.e.,
theoretical analysis, might explain why a particular
piece of music is the way it is, i.e., how it is
constructed. What it will not do is demonstrate the
humanistic and cultural aspects that make music the
expressive medium that it is. The broader aspects of
hermeneutical analysis are denied the musicologist if
he remain only on the level of theoretical analysis.
Musicology, if it is to be a force in the life of
musicians, must embrace both aspects of description and
interpretation.

However, before music is subjected to analysis of
whatever ilk, the musicologists should be guided by the
following fundamental principle: first experience the
music, then reflect. After all, music is the core of
musicology, all else is ancillary.

b. Musicologisms

When these ancillary matters take on a life and
importance of their own and usurp the musical core of
musicology they are called musicologisms. The most
insidious of these musicologisms is biography and the
results of necropsychiatry. There are few objections to
be raised about biography and psychological profiles as
pastime, but when they are used as the tool for the
aesthetic and critical analysis of music they run the very
great risk of putting the musicologist in the position of
committing the intentional fallacy, which is to judge,
evaluate and interpret a work of art using the intentions

of the artist as the analytical tool. Under this rubric,
aesthetic and critical arguments and evaluations are
backwards and violate the first principle of musicology
laid down in the previous section. It is of dubious value
to argue from the supposed intentions of a composer, alive
or dead, to the evaluation, on whatever level, of a piece
of music. Any and all musicological arguments must move
in the other direction--start with the experience of the
music itself; then evaluate, criticize, analyze, etc.

Another area prone to produce musicologisms is that
of theoretical analysis. The danger here, it seems to
me, is the desire to "universalize" a system of analysis
and then use that system as an evaluative tool for the
whole body of music. For example: it is one thing to
generalize about the formal makeup of the classical
symphony, it is another to universalize that formal
structure and maintain that all pieces of music called
"symphony" must conform to the classical model in order
to be pronounced "good." This tendency to absolutize is
also evident in some schools of harmonic analysis. The
harmonic language of Western music is a volatile thing.
To set up one particular moment in that language's
development as the paradigm and criterion of judgment
for another time period is to produce a musicologism--
the paradigm has become the kat' exochen and not the
music.

Finally, in the area of aesthetics and criticism
this propensity to musicologize is very evident. Quite
often much of the music of the 20th century and much
older music is judged "bad" or inferior because the
standards of judgment being employed were devised for

the aesthetics of the 19th century. When an aesthetic
theory is thus absolutized it becomes cast in intellectual
cement and becomes much more important and insidious than
the experience of the music itself. We then have a
musicologism.

c. Historical-systematic

As we saw in the retrospective, the division of
musicology into historical and systematic areas has a
long history going back to the division of ancient Greek
music into its speculative and practical aspects.
Aristides Quintilianus <5.a.6> was the first of the
writers surveyed dualistically to schematize music and
he was merely following a tradition going back through
Ptolemy to Aristoxenus. When Guido Adler wrote his
seminal article on musicology in 1885 he included his
version of Aristides Quintilianus' schema which is that
that now divides musicology. It seems more in keeping
with the phenomenon under scrutiny, i.e., musicology,
that the traditional division is unwarranted. Both
Forkel and Charles Seeger are on a track that more
adequately conforms to the history and critique of the
field of musicology: musicology is a unified discipline
not a divided one. Each of the regions within the field
of musicology has its own history, indeed histories have
been written of some of these regions. Nevertheless,
the entity "musicology" has been multiplied beyond need
by Guido Adler.

One can understand why the ancients thought of
music in dualistic terms. Music had a dual purpose:

voice of the cosmic harmony and for mere enjoyment and
pleasure, although one did not write much about the
mundane side of music. That Medieval writers took only
from the speculative side of ancient music theory is
also understandable--it is what they inherited from
Boëthius. However, after the 10th century music
treatises took a practical turn because of the desire
for an adequate notation system and for teaching
purposes. When we come to the Renaissance we find a
fusion of ancient speculative music theory and Renaissance practice (inherited from the Middle Ages) which was
given to the Enlightenment as the "new" music theory. It
is at this point that history, as we know it, began. But
it was a history of what had become musical practice in
the Renaissance. Enter Forkel: history is the channel
through which flows the art of music in all its aspects
and the flux of these events is assumed. Music and
writing on music was a unified field for Forkel, superimposed on the historical flux. Strange as it may seem,
Guido Adler ignores Forkel and imposes on the new
discipline of musicology a schema that forces it into an
ancient model, the usefulness and purposes for which it
was devised being long dead.

Finally, putting aside this ancient dual model that
does not adequately serve the purposes of modern musicology, the discipline should be seen as a broad area of
study, not just historical, that contains within it the
regions of historical studies; music theory; music education and pedagogy; aesthetics; etc. Common goals,
e.g., the study and understanding of music in its
cultural context, could be pursued by workers in a
unified, not a fragmented field.

NOTES FOR CHAPTER IV

[1]The numbers written thus <2.a> refer to section and subsections in the retrospective.

[2]Iannis Xenakis, Formalized Music: Thought and Mathematics in Composition (Bloomington: Indiana University Press, 1971).

[3]Adler, "Umfang, Methode...," p. 8.

[4]Hans Heinz Dräger, "Musikwissenschaft," Universitas litterarum: Handbuch der Wissenschaftkunde (Berlin: W. de Gruyter, 1955), p. 635.

[5]Charles Seeger, Studies in Musicology: 1935-1975 (Berkeley: University of California Press, 1977), p. 3.

[6]Adler, "Umfang, Methode...," p. 11.

[7]Seeger, Studies in Musicology, pp. 1-15.

[8]Walter Wiora, Historische und systematische Musikwissenschaft (Tutzing: H. Schneider, 1972).

[9]Wilibad Gurlitt, Musikgeschichte und Gegenwart (Wiesbaden: Steiner, 1966-   ).

[10]Arnold Schering, Handbuch der Musikgeschichte (Hildesheim: Georg Olms, 1976). See also his Bachs Textbehandlung (Leipzig: Kahnt, 1900).

[11]Henry Paul Lang, Music in Western Civilization (New York: W. W. Norton, 1941).

[12]Donald Grout, A History of Western Music, 3rd ed. (New York: W. W. Norton, 1980).

[13]Richard L. Crocker, History of Musical Style (New York: McGraw-Hill Book Co., 1966).

[14]Hans Heinrich Eggebrecht, ed., Handwörterbuch der musikalischen Terminologie (Wiesbaden: F. Steiner, 1972-   ).

[15]Stanley Sadie, ed., The New Grove Dictionary of Music and Musicians (London: Macmillan Publishers, Ltd., 1980).

[16]Friedrich Blume, ed., Die Musik in Geschichte und Gegenwart (Kassel: Bärenreiter, 1949-1951).

[17]Nicolas Slonimsky, ed., Baker's Biographical Dictionary of Musicians, 6th ed. (New York: Schirmer, 1978).

[18]W. W. Cobbett, Cobbett's Cyclopedic Survey of Chamber Music, 2nd ed. (London: Oxford University Press, 1963).

[19]Curt Sachs, Real-Lexikon der Musikinstrumente (New York: Dover Publications, 1964).

[20]Carl Parrish, The Notation of Mediaeval Music (New York: W. W. Norton, 1957).

[21]Willi Apel, Notation of Polyphonic Music, 900-1600, 5th ed. (Cambridge: Mediaeval Academy of America, 1961).

[22]Johannes Wolf, Geschichte der Mensural-Notation von 150-1460 (Wiesbaden: Breitkopf & Härtel, 1904).

[23]J. Chailley, Les Notations musicales nouvelles (Paris: A. Leduc, 1950).

[24]Leon Dallin, Techniques of Twentieth-Century Composition, 3rd ed. (Dubuque: Wm. C. Brown Co. Pub., 1974).   There is no one section on notation in this volume, each chapter contains notational material within the body of the text.

[25]Reginald Smith Brindle, The New Music (London: Oxford University Press, 1975), pp. 188-198; electronic music notation, pp. 105-107.

[26]Gary E. Wittlich, ed., Aspects of Twentieth-Century Music (Englewood Cliffs: Prentice-Hall, Inc., 1975), pp. 263-269).

[27]Kurt Stone, Music Notation in the Twentieth Century (New York: W. W. Norton, 1980).

[28]Odo of Cluny, Quomodo organistrum construatur and De fistulis, in Jacques Paul Migne, Patriologiae Cursus Completus (Latina) (Parisiis: J. P. Migne, 1844-1864), CXXXIII, pp. 815-816.

[29]Adler, "Umfang, Methode...," p. 10.

[30]Sachs, Real-Lexikon der Musikinstrumente.

[31]Adler, "Umfang, Methode...," pp. 9-10.

[32]Arnold Dolmetsch, The Interpretation of the Music of the XVIIth and XVIIIth Centuries Revealed by Contemporary Evidence (London: Novello, 1915).

[33]Adolf Beyschlag, Die Ornamentik der Musik (Leipzig: Breitkopf & Härtel, 1953).

[34]Robert Donington, The Interpretation of Early Music, New Version (New York: St. Martin's Press, 1974).

[35]Michael B. Collins, The Performance of Coloration, Sesquialtera, and Hemiolia (1450-1750) (Ph.D. dissertation, Stanford University, 1963).

[36]Anna H. Heyer, Historical Sets, Collected Editions, and Monuments of Music, 3rd ed. (Chicago: American Library Association, 1980).

[37]Zarlino, Istitutione Harmoniche, i, 3.

[38]Adler, "Umfang, Methode...," pp. 11-13; 17.

[39]Ibid., 13.

[40]Michael L. Mark, Contemporary Music Education (New York: Schirmer Books, 1978), p. 96.

[41]Carl Orff and Gunild Keetman, Orff-Schulwerk (Mainz: B. Schott's Söhne, 1955).

[42]Adler, "Umfang, Methode..., p. 17.

[43]Ibid., p. 14.

[44]Jaap Kunst, Ethno-musicology, 2nd ed. (St. Claire Shores: Scholarly Press, 1977).

[45]Bruno Nettl, Theory and Method in Ethnomusicology (The Free Press of Glencoe, 1964), pp. 5-7.

[46]Ibid., p. 9.

[47]Mantle Hood, The Ethnomusicologist (New York: McGraw-Hill Book Co., 1971), pp. 25-49.

[48]Nettl, Theory and Method in Ethnomusicology, p. 10.

[49]Arnold Schoenberg, Fundamentals of Musical Composition (London: Faber and Faber, Ltd., 1967).

[50]Paul Hindemith, Craft of Musical Composition (New York: Associated Music Pub., Inc., 1945).

[51]Oliver Messiaen, The Technique of My Musical Language, trans. John Satterfield (Paris: A. Leduc, 1956).

[52]Iannis Xenakis, Formalized Music: Thought and Mathematics in Composition (Bloomington: Indiana University Press, 1971).

[53]Heinrich Schenker, Neue musikalishe Theorien und Phantasien (Wien: Universal Edition, 1906).

[54]Allen Forte, The Structure of Atonal Music (New York: Yale University Press, 1973).

[55]Adler, "Umfang, Methode..., p. 10.

[56]Dika Newlin, "The 'Mahler's Brother Syndrome': Necropsychiatry and the Artist," Musical Quarterly 66 (1980):   296-304.

BIBLIOGRAPHY

Adkins, Cecil. "The Theory and Practice of the
Monochord." Ph.D. dissertation, University of
Iowa, 1963.

Adler, Guido. "Umfang, Methode und Ziel der
Musikwissenschaft," Vierteljahresshcrift für Musikwissenschaft 1 (1885): 5-20.

Ambros, August. The Boundaries of Music and Poetry.
Translated by J. H. Cornell. New York: G.
Schirmer, 1893.

_____. Geschichte der Musik. Leipzig:
Leuckart, 1880.

Apel, Willi, ed. Harvard Dictionary of Music. 2nd ed.
Cambridge: Harvard University Press, 1969.

_____. Notation of Polyphonic Music, 900-1600.
5th ed. Cambridge: Mediaeval Academy of America,
1961.

<Aristotle>. Problems. Translated by W. S. Hett.
Cambridge: Harvard University Press, 1970.

Aristotle. The Works of Aristotle. Various
    translators. Chicago: Encyclopaedia Britannica,
    Inc., 1952.

Aristoxenus. Harmonics. Translated by Henry S.
    Macran. Oxford: Clarendon Press, 1902.

Aron, Pietro. Libri Tres de Institutione harmonica.
    Bologna: Forni, 1970.

_____. Toscanello in Music. Translated by
    Peter Bergquist. Colorado Springs: Colorado
    College Music Press.

Athenaeus. The Deipnosophists. Translated by C. B.
    Gulick, Cambridge: Harvard University Press, 1937.

Augustine. De Musica. In J. P. Migne, Patrologiae
    Cursus Completus (Latina). Parisiis: J. P. Migne,
    1844-1864.

Babb, W. Hucbald, Guido, and John on Music: Three
    Mediaeval Treatises. Edited by Claude Palisca.
    New Haven: Yale University Press, 1979.

Beyschlag, Adolf. Die Ornamentik der Musik. Leipzig:
    Breitkopf & Härtel, 1953.

Blume, Friedrich, ed. Die Musik in Geschichte und
    Gegenwart. Kassel: Bärenreiter, 1949-1951.

_____. Renaissance and Baroque Music. New
    York: W. W. Norton & Co., Inc., 1967.

Boëthius. De Institutione Arithmetica, libri duo. De
    Institutione Musica, libri quinque. Edited by
    G. Friedlein. Lipsiae, 1867.

_____. Topicorum Aristotelis Interpretatio. In J.
    P. Migne, Patrologiae Cursus Completus (Latina).
    Parisiis: J. P. Migne, 1844-1864.

Bower, Calvin M. "Boëthius' The Principles of Music, an
    Introduction, Translation, and Commentary," Ph.D.
    dissertation. George Peabody College of Teachers,
    1966.

Brindle, Reginald Smith. The New Music. London:
    Oxford University Press, 1975.

Bukofzer, Manfred F. Music in the Baroque Era. New
    York: W. W. Norton, 1947.

Cassiodorus. De Artibus ac Disciplina Liberalium
    Litterarum. De Musica. In J. P. Migne,
    Patrologiae Cursus Completus (Latina). Parisiis:
    J. P. Migne, 1844-1864.

_____. Variae. In J. P. Migne, Patrologiae
    Cursus Completus (Latina). Parisiis: J. P. Migne,
    1844-1864.

Censorius. De Die Natali. In Johannes Sichardus,
    comp. Disciplinarum Liberalium Orbis. Basileae:
    Johan. Beleius, 1528.

Chailley, J. Les Notations musicales nouvelles. Paris:
    A. Leduc, 1950.

Chrysander, Friedrich, ed. Jahrbücher für musikalische-
    Wissenschaft. Leipzig: 1863, 1867.

Cobbett, W. W. Cobbett's Cyclopedic Survey of Chamber
    Music. 2nd ed. London: Oxford University Press,
    1963.

Collins, Michael B. "The Performance of Coloration,
    Sesquialtera, and Hemiolia (1450-1750)." Ph.D.
    dissertation, Stanford University, 1963.

Coussemaker, E., ed. Scriptorum de musica medii aevi.
    Paris: A. Durand, 1864-1876.

Crocker, Richard L. History of Musical Style. New
    York: McGraw-Hill Book Co., 1966.

Dallin, Leon. Techniques of Twentieth-Century
    Composition. 3rd ed. Dubuque: Wm. C. Brown Co.,
    Pub., 1974.

Deferrari, R. J. The Fathers of the Church. New York:
    Fathers of the Church, Inc., 1947.

Descartes, René. Compendium of Music. Translated by
    Walter Robert. American Institute of Musicology,
    1964.

_____. _Discourse_ _on_ _Method_. Translated by
    Elizabeth Haldane and G. R. T. Ross. Chicago:
    Encyclopaedia Britannica, Inc., 1952.

_____. _Meditations_. Translated by Elizabeth
    Haldane and G. R. T. Ross. Chicago: Encyclopaedia
    Britannica, Inc., 1952.

Diehl, E. _Anthologia_ _Lyrica_ _Graeca_. Leipzig: 1942.

Diogenes Laertius. _Lives_ _of_ _Eminent_ _Philosophers_.
    Translated by R. D. Hicks. Cambridge: Harvard
    University Press, 1972.

Dolmetsch, Arnold. _The_ _Interpretation_ _of_ _the_ _Music_ _of_
    the _XVIIth_ _and_ _SVIIIth_ _Centuries_ _Revealed_ _by_
    Contemporary _Evidence_. London: Novello, 1915.

Donington, Robert. _The_ _Interpretation_ _of_ _Early_ _Music_.
    New version. New York: St. Martin's Press, 1974.

Dräger, Hans Heinz. "Musikwissenschaft." _Universitas_
    litterarum: _Handbuch_ _der_ _Wissenschaftkunde_,
    p. 635. Berlin: W. de Gruyter, 1955.

Durant, Will. _The_ _Life_ _of_ _Greece_. New York: Simon and
    Schuster, 1939.

Eggebrecht, Hans Heinrich, ed. _Handwörterbuch_ _der_
    musikalischen _Terminologie_. Wiesbaden: F.
    Steiner, 1972- .

Einstein, Alfred. Music in the Romantic Era. New York:
    W. W. Norton, 1947.

Eitner, Robert. Bibliographie der Musik-Sammelwerke des
    XVI. und XVII. Jahrhunderts. Berlin: 1877.

_____. Biographisch-Bibliographisches Quellen-
    Lexikon der Musiker und Musikgelehrten der
    christlichen Zeitrechnung bis zur Mitte der
    neunzehnten Jahrhunderts. Leipzig: Breitkopf &
    Härtel, 1900-1904.

Farmer, George Henry. Historical Facts for the Arabian
    Musical Influence. London: William Reeves, s.d.

_____. "The Music of Islam." In New
    Oxford History of Music, I, pp. 421-477. London:
    Oxford University Press, 1957.

Fétis, François-Joseph. Biographie Universelle des
    Musiciens. 2nd ed. Paris: Didot, 1873.

_____. Histoire Générale de la
    Musique. Paris: Didot, 1869.

_____. Méthode des Méthodes de Chant.
    Paris: 1869.

_____ and Ignaz Moscheles. Méthode des
    Méthodes de Piano. Paris: 1840.

_____. Traité de la theorie et de la
practique de l'harmonie. Paris: M. Schlesinger,
1844.

_____. Traité du contrepoint et de la
fugue. Paris: Janet & Cotells, 1824.

Forkel, Johann Nicolaus. Allgemeine Geschichte der
Musik. Leipzig: Schwickertschen Verlag, 1788,
1801.

_____. Allgemeine Litteratur der
Musik, Leipzig: 1792.

_____. Johann Sebastian Bach His
Life, Art, and Work. Translated by Charles S.
Terry. London: Constable and Co., Ltd., 1920.

_____. Ueber die Theorie der Musik,
insofern sie Liebhabern und Kennern nothwendig und
nützlich ist. Göttingen: im Verlag der Wittwe
Vandenhück, 1777.

Forte, Allen. The Structure of Atonal Music. New York:
Yale University Press, 1973.

Franck, Wolf. "Musicology and its founder, J. N.
Forkel." Musical Quarterly 35 (1949): 588-601.

Franco of Cologne. Ars Cantus Mensurabilis. Edited by
Gilbert Reany and A. Gilles. American Institute of
Musicology, 1974.

Fux, Johann Josef. Gradus ad Parnassum. Vienna:
    Joannis Petri van Ghelen, 1725.

Galilei, Galileo. Two New Sciences. Translated by
    Stillman Drake. Madison: The University of
    Wisconsin Press, 1974.

Gerbert, Martin. Scriptores Ecclesiastici de Musica
    Sacra Potissimum. Hildesheim: Georg Olms, 1963.

Glarean, Heinrich. Dodecachordon. Translated by
    Clement A. Miller. American Institute of
    Musicology, 1965.

_____. Isagoge in Musicen. Translated by
    Frances Berry Turrell. Journal of Music Theory 3
    (1959): 97-139.

_____. Musicae Epitome sive Compendium ex
    Glareani Dodecachordo. Basel: Heinrich Petri,
    1557. Grabmann, Marin. Geschichte der
    scholastischen Methode. Freiberg im Breisgau,
    1909.

Grout, Donald. A History of Western Music. 3rd ed.
    New York: W. W. Norton, 1980.

Grube, G. M. A. Plato's Thought. Boston: Beacon
    Press, 1958.

Guido d'Arezzo. Epistola de ignoto cantu. In Martin
    Gerbert. Scriptores Ecclesiastici de Musica Sacra
    Potissimum. Hildesheim: Georg Olms, 1963.

_____. Micrologus. In Martin Gerbert.
    Scriptores Ecclesiastici de Musica Sacra
    Potissimum. Hildesheim: Georg Olms, 1963.

_____. Regulae musicae de ignoto cantu. In
    Martin Gerbert. Scriptores Ecclesiastici de Musica
    Sacra Potissimum. Hildesheim: Georg Olms, 1963.

Gurlitt, Wilibald. Musikgeschichte und Gegenwart.
    Wiesbaden: Steiner, 1966- .

Guthrie, W. K. C. A History of Greek Philosophy.
    Cambridge: Cambridge University Press, 1962.

Hanslick, Eduard. Vom Musikalisch-schönen. Wiesban:
    Breitkopf & Härtel, 1978.

Harriss, Ernest Charles. "Johann Mattheson's Der
    vollkomene Capellmeister: a Translation and
    Commentary." Ph.D. dissertation, George Peabody
    College for Teachers, 1969.

Hauptmann, Moritz. The Nature of Harmony and Meter.
    Translated by W. E. Heathcote. London: Swan
    Sonenschein & Co., 1888.

Hawkins, John. A General History of the Science and
    Practice of Music. London: Novello, 1853.

Helmholtz, Hermann von. The Mechanism of the Ossicles
    of the Ear and Membrana Tympani. Translated by
    A. H. Buck and N. Smith. New York: William Wood &
    Co., 1873.

_____. On the Sensations of Tone as a
    Physiological Basis for the Theory of Music.
    Translated by Alexander J. Ellis. New York: Dover
    Publications, Inc., 1954.

Henderson, Isobel. "Ancient Greek Music." In New
    Oxford History of Music, I, pp. 336-403. London:
    Oxford University Press, 1957.

Heyer, Anna H. Historical Sets, Collected Editions, and
    Monuments of Music. 3rd ed. Chicago: American
    Library Association, 1980.

Hindemith, Paul. Craft of Musical Composition. New
    York: Associated Music Pub., Inc., 1945.

Hood, Mantle. The Ethnomusicologist. New York:
    McGraw-Hill Book Co., 1971.

Huglo, Michael. Les Tonaires. Paris: Société
    Française de Musicologie, 1971.

Husserl, Edmund. Crisis of European Sciences and
    Transcendental Phenomenology. Translated by David
    Carr. Evanston: Northwestern University Press,
    1970.

_____. Formal and Transcendental Logic.
    Translated by Dorian Cairns. The Hague: Martinus
    Nijhoff, 1969.

Iamblichus. Nikomachi Arithmeticam Introductionem.
    Lipsiae: Teuboneri, 1894.

Isidore of Seville. De Ecclesiasticis Officiis. In
    J. P. Migne. Patrologiae Cursus Completus
    (Latina). Parisiis: J. P. Migne, 1844-1864.

_____. Etymologiarum sive originum, libri
    XX. De Musica. Edited by W. M. Lindsay. Oxonii:
    Clarendoniano, 1911.

Jan, Karl von. Musici Scriptores Graeci. Lipsiae:
    Teubneri, 1895.

Johannes, monk of Cluny. St. Odo of Cluny. Translated
    by Dom Gerard Sitwell. London: Sheed and Ward,
    1958.

Johannes de Garlandia. Concerning Measured Music.
    Translated by Stanley H. Birnbaum. Colorado
    Springs: Colorado College Music Press, 1978.

_____. De Mensurabili Musica. Edited
    by Erich Reimer. Wiesbaden: Franz Steiner, 1972.

John Cotton. Musica. In Martin Gerbert, Scriptores
    Ecclesiastici de Musica Sacra Potissimum.
    Hildesheim: George Olms, 1963.

_____. De Musica Cum Tonario. Edited by J. Smits
    van Waesberghe. Rome: American Institute of
    Musicology, 1950.

John Scotus Eriugena. De Divisione Naturae. In J. P.
    Migne. Patrologiae Cursus Completus (Latina).
    Parisiis: J. P. Migne, 1844-1864.

Kahl, Alexis. Die Philosophie der Musik nach
    Aristoteles. Leipzig: Breitkopf & Härtel, 1902.

Kant, Immanuel. Critique of Pure Reason. Translated by
    Norman Kemp Smith. New York: St. Martin's Press,
    1965.

Köchel, Ludwig von. Johann Josef Fux. Vienna: Hölder,
    1972.

Krenek, Ernest. "Proportionem und pythagoräische
    Hämmer." Musica 14 (1960): 708-712.

Kretzschmar, Hermann. "Anregungen zur Förderung
    musikalischer Hermeneutik." Gesammelte Aufsätze
    aus den Jahrbüchern der Musikbibliothek Peters,
    vol. 2. Leipzig: C. F. Peters, 1911.

_____. Führer durch den Konzertsaal.
    Leipzig: Breitkopf & Härtel, 1888-1890.

_____. Kleine Handbücher der
    Musikgeschichte nach Gattungen. Leipzig:
    Breitkopf & Härtel, 1919.

Kunst, Jaap. Ethno-musicology. 2nd ed. St. Claire
    Shores: Scholarly Press, 1977.

Kuttner, Fritz A. Bericht über siebenten
    internationalen musikwissenschaftlichen Kongress,
    Köln 1958.

Lang, Paul Henry. _Music in Western Civilization_. New
    York: W. W. Norton, 1941.

Lohmann, Johannes. _Musiké und Logos_. Stuttgart:
    Musikwissenschaftliche Verlags-Gesellschaft m.b.H.,
    1970.

McDermott, Albin Dunstan. "The '_Micrologus_' of Guido
    d'Arezzo." Master's thesis. University of
    Pittsburgh, 1929.

Mann, Alfred. _Steps to Parnassus: The Study of
    Counterpoint_. New York: W. W. Norton & Co., Inc.,
    1943.

_____. _The Study of Fugue_. New Brunswick, N. J.:
    Rutgers University Press, 1958.

Mark, Michael L. _Contemporary Music Education_. New
    York: Schirmer Books, 1978.

Marpurg, Friedrich. _Abhandlung von der Fuge_. Berlin:
    A. Haude und J. C. Spener, 1753.

_____. _Die Kunst das Clavier zu Spielen_.
    Berlin: A. Haude und J. C. Spener, 1762.

Marquard, Paul, ed. _Die harmonischen Fragmente des
    Aristoxenus_. Berlin: Wiedmannsche Buchhandlung,
    1868.

Martianus Capella. _De Nuptiis Philologiae et Mercurii_.
    Edited by A. Dick. Leipzig: Teubner, 1925.

Mason, John Hope. The Indispensable Rousseau. London:
    Quartet Books, 1979.

Mattheson, Johann. Exemplarische Organisten-Probe.
    Hamburg: Im Schiller und Kissnerischen Buchladen,
    1719.

_____. Das forschende Orchestre. Hamburg:
    B. Schillers Wittwe und J. C. Kissner, 1721.

_____. Grundlage einer Ehrenpfore.
    Hamburg: In verlegung des Verfassers, 1740.

_____. Kleine und Grosse General-Bass-
    Schule. Hamburg: J. C. Kissner, 1735.

_____. Das neu eröffnete Orchestre.
    Hamburg: bey Benjamin Schillers Wittwe im Thum,
    1713.

Maxham, Robert E. "The Contributions of Joseph Sauveur
    (1653-1767) to acoustics." Ph.D. dissertation,
    Eastman School of Music, 1976.

Meibom, Marcus. Antiquae musicae auctores septem.
    Amstelodami: apud Ludovicum Elzevirium, 1652.

Mersenne, Marin. Harmonicorum instrumentorum libri IV.
    Paris: Guillaume Baudry, 1635-1636, 1648.

_____. Harmonie Universelle. Paris: S.
    Cramoisy, 1636-1637.

Messiaen, Olivier. The Technique of My Musical
    Language. Translated by John Satterfield. Paris:
    A. Leduc, 1956.

Migne, Jacques Paul. Patrologiae Cursus Completus
    (Latina). Parisiis: J. P. Migne, 1844-1864.

Mill, John Stuart. A System of Logic. London:
    Longmans, Green, 1961.

Musica Enchiriadis. In Martin Gerbert. Scriptores
    Ecclesiastici de Musica Sacra Potissimum.
    Hildesheim: George Olms, 1963.

Nettl, Bruno. Theory and Method in Ethnomusicology.
    The Free Press of Glencoe, 1964.

New Grove Dictionary of Music and Musicians. 1980 ed.
    S.v. "Vitry, Philippe de," by Ernest H. Sanders.

Newlin, Dika. "The 'Mahler's Brother Syndrome':
    Necropsychiatry and the Artist." Musical Quarterly
    66 (1980): 296-304.

Odo of Cluny. Dialogus de Musica. In Martin Gerbert.
    Scriptores Ecclesiastici de Musica Sacra
    Potissimum. Hildesheim: Georg Olms, 1963.

_____. De Fistulis. In Jacques Paul Migne.
    Patrologiae Cursus Completus (Latina). Parisiis:
    J. P. Migne, 1844-1864.

_____. Quomodo organistrum construatur. In
Jacques Paul Migne, Patrologiae Cursus Completus
(Latina). Parisiis: J. P. Migne, 1844-1864.

Orff, Carl and Gunild Keetman. Orff-Schulwerk. Mainz:
B. Schott's Söhne, 1955.

Papakhian, Arsen Ralph. "Jean-Philippe Rameau's
Demonstration du Principe de l'harmonie (1750) and
Pierre Esteve's Nouvelles Decouverts du Principe de
l'harmonie (1752): a Translation." M. M. thesis,
Western Michigan University, 1973.

Parrish, Carl. The Notation of Mediaeval Music. New
York: W. W. Norton, 1957.

Philippe de Vitry. Ars Nova. Edited by Gilbert Reany.
American Institute of Musicology, 1964.

_____. Ars Nova. Translated by Leon
Plantinga. Journal of Music Theory 5 (1961): 204-
223.

Philo Judaeus. Philo. Translated by F. H. Colson and
G. H. Whitaker. Cambridge: Harvard University
Press, 1929-62.

Plato. The Dialogues of Plato. Translated by Benjamin
Jowett. Chicago: Encyclopaedia Brittanica, Inc.,
1952.

Pöhlmann, Egert. Denkmäler altgriechischer Musik:
    Sammlung, Übertragung und Erläuterung aller
    Fragmente und Fälschungen. Nürnberg: Hans Carl,
    1970.

Ptolemy. Harmonikon. Edited by Ingemar Düring.
    Göteborg: Elanders Boktyckeri Aktiebolag, 1930.

Rameau, Jean-Philippe. Origine des sciences, suivie
    d'une controverse sur le même sujet. Paris: 1762.

_____. Treatise on Harmony. Translated
    by Philip Gossett. New York: Dover Publications,
    Inc., 1971.

Reese, Gustave. Music in the Middle Ages. New York:
    W. W. Norton & Co., 1940.

Regino of Prüm. De Harmonica Institutione. In J. P.
    Migne, Patrologiae Cursus Completus (Latina).
    Parisiis: J. P. Migne, 1844-1864.

Riemann, Hugo. Grundriss der Musikwissenschaft.
    Leipzig: Quelle & Meyer, 1928.

_____. History of Music Theory. Translated by
    Raymond H. Haggh. Lincoln: University of Nebraska
    Press, 1962.

_____. Hugo Riemann's Theory of Harmony and
History of Music Theory, Book III. Translated and
    edited by William C. Mickelsen. Lincoln:
    University of Nebraska Press, 1977.

_____. Kleines Handbuch der Musikgeschichte mit
Periodisierung nach Stil prinzipien und Formen.
5th ed. Leipzig: Breitkopf & Härtel, 1932.

_____. Musik Lexikon. 11th ed. Berlin: Max
Hesses Verlag, 1929.

_____. "The Nature of Harmony." In New Lessons
in Harmony, by John Comfort Fillmore.
Philadelphia: T. Presser, 1887.

_____. Studien zur Geschichte der Notenschrift.
Leipzig: Breitkopf & Härtel, 1878.

_____. Vereinfachte Harmonielehre. London:
Augner and Co., 1893.

Rousseau, Jean-Jacques. Oeuvres complètes de J. J.
Rousseau. Paris: Furne et Cie., 1837.

_____. Oeuvres de J. J. Rousseau.
Paris: Werdet et Lequien Fils, 1826.

Sachs, Curt. Real-Lexikon der Musikinstrumente. New
York: Dover Publications, 1964.

Sadie, Stanley, ed. The New Grove Dictionary of Music
and Musicians. London: Macmillan Publishers,
Ltd., 1980.

Sauveur, Joseph. Mémoires de l'Académie Royale des
Sciences. Amsterdam: Chez Pierre Mortier, 1701-
1713.

Schenker, Heinrich. Neue musikalisch Theorien und
    Phantasien. Wien: Universal Edition, 1906.

Scherchen, Hermann. The Nature of Music. Henry Regnery
    Co., 1950.

Schering, Arnold. Bachs Textbehandlung. Leipzig:
    Kahnt, 1900.

_____. Handbuch der Musikgeschichte.
    Hildesheim: Georg Olms, 1976.

Schoenberg, Arnold. Fundamentals of Musical
    Composition. London: Faber and Faber, Ltd., 1967.

Seeger, Charles. Studies in Musicology: 1935-1975.
    Berkeley: University of California Press, 1977.

Slonimsky, Nicolas, ed. Baker's Biographical Dictionary
    of Musicians. 6th ed. New York: Schirmer, 1978.

Stahl, W. H. Martianus Capella and the Seven Liberal
    Arts. New York: Columbia University Press, 1977.

Stevenson, Robert. "The Rivals Hawkins, Burney and
    Boswell." Musical Quarterly 36 (1950): 67-82.

Stone, Kurt. Music Notation in the Twentieth Century.
    New York: W. W. Norton, 1980.

Strunk, W. O. Source Readings in Music History. New
    York: W. W. Norton, 1950.

Tatarkiewicz, Władysław. History of Aesthetics.
Warszawa: PWN-Polish Scientific Publishers, 1970.

Tinctoris, Johannes. The Art of Counterpoint (Liber de
Arte Contrapuncti). Translated by Albert Seay.
American Institute of Musicology, 1961.

_____. Complexus Effectum Musices. In E.
de Coussemaker. Scriptorum de musica medii aevi.
Paris: A. Durand, 1864-1876.

_____. Dictionary of Musical Terms
(Terminorum Musicae Diffinitorium). Translated by
Carl Parrish. London: Collier-Macmillan, Ltd.,
1963.

Vered, Cohen. "Zarlino on Modes." Ph.D. dissertation,
City University of New York, 1967.

Vicentino, Nicola. L'Antica Musica Ridotta alla Moderna
Prattica. Rome: 1555; reprint ed. Kassel:
Bärenreiter, 1959.

Waesberghe, J. Smits van. Guidonis Aretini Micrologus.
American Institute of Musicology, 1955.

_____. Guidonis "Prologus in
Antiphonarium." Buren: Frits Knuf, 1975.

Waite, William G. "Johannes de Garlandia, poet and
musician." Speculum 35 (1960): 179-195.

Weinmann, Karl. Johannes Tinctoris und sein unbekannter
    Traktat "De inventione et usu musicae." Tutzing:
    Hans Schneider, 1961.

Wiora, Walter. Historische und systematische
    Musikwissenschaft. Tutzing: H. Schneider, 1972.

Wittlich, Gary E., ed. Aspects of Twentieth-Century
    Music. Englewood Cliffs: Prentice-Hall, Inc.,
    1975.

Wolf, Johannes. Geschichte der Mensural-Notation von
    1250-1460. Wiesbaden: Breitkopf & Härtel, 1904.

Xenakis, Iannis. Formalized Music: Thought and
    Mathematics in Composition. Bloomington: Indiana
    University Press, 1971.

Zarlino, Gioseffo. The Art of Counterpoint. Translated
    by Guy A. Marco and Claude V. Palisca. New Haven:
    Yale University Press, 1968.

_____. Dimonstrati Harmoniche. Venice,
    1571; reprint ed., Farnborough: Gregg Press, 1966.

_____. Le Istitutioni Harmonische. Venice:
    Francesco Senese, 1562.

_____. Sopplimento Musicali. Venice, 1588;
    reprint ed., Ridgewood: Gregg Press, 1966.

APPENDIX I

J.N. FORKEL'S MUSICOLOGICAL SCHEMA

I. The physical theory of sound

    this explains:

    a,   the method of origin of sound in general
    b,   the method of various kinds of the same in
          particular
    c,   duration; and
    d,   the spread and propagation of the same
    e,   reverberation (echo) along with the various
          kinds of the same;
    f,   sympathy of tones
    g,   acoustic phenomena

II. Mathematical theory of sound

    this teaches:

    a,   the measuring out of the sizes of pitches (in
          general);
    b,   their formation <in->to regular tones and
          measured <off> intervals in particular,
    c,   the various kinds of intervals;

d,   the influence of the physical and
      mathematical theory of sound on the
      construction of instruments, along with
      remarks about the nature of the most-known
      instrumental genres.

III. Musical grammar

      this teaches:

A.   musical symbol theory

      a,   the system of lines, on and between which
            the actual symbols of sounds are placed;
      b,   the clefs to the system of lines,
            alongside the natural causes of their
            difference;
      c,   the notes as actual symbols of the tones,
            insofar as they designate the pitch and
            duration of these;
      d,   the silence symbols; (rests)
      e,   sharp, flat, natural, and repeat signs;
      f,   the arcs, strokes and dots, alongside
            everything which additionally belongs
            <there>to designating a musical thought
            for the face <=eye> exactly in a way that
            it should be made audible to the ear by
            the performance.

B.   The musical keys <u>Tonarten</u> (scales, gamuts, modes)

    a,   the number of musical intervals
    b,   their difference with respect to concord or discord;
    c,   the sound of tone classes;
    d,   the scales and keys formed from these;
    e,   the characteristics of the tones belonging in these scales;

C.   The theory of harmony

    a,   the harmonic triad;
    b,   the essential seventh chord;
    c,   the consonant harmonies deriving from the harmonic triad;
    d,   the dissonant harmonies deriving from the principal 7th chord;
    e,   the retardation and anticipation of harmonies;
    f,   modulation, or progression and connection of harmonies;
    g,   harmonic cadences;
    h,   foreign deviations. (Chromatics)

D.   Musical prosody. (Rhythmopoeia.)

    a,   accents;
    b,   musical feet; <as in poetry!>
    c,   meters;
    d,   sectional verses;

IV. Musical rhetoric

     this teaches:

     A.   Musical periodology
          a,   rhythmical
          b,   logical; and then as either
          c,   homophonic; or
          d,   polyphonic

     B.   The musical styles

          a,   church style;
          b,   chamber style;
          c,   theater style;

     C.   The musical genres

          a,   choruses;
          b,   terzets;
          c,   duets;
          d,   arias;
          e,   recitative;
          f,   fugue;
          g,   overtures;
          h,   the symphony;
          i,   the sonata;
          j,   the concerto;
          k,   the characteristic French dance melodies,
               etc.

D.   The aesthetic arrangement of musical ideas

    1. a,   <sic> the theme;
       b,   auxiliary phrases;
       c,   counter phrases;
       d,   subdivisions;
       e,   exordium;
       f,   proposition;
       g,   refutation;
       h,   affirmation;
       i,   conclusion;

    2. the rhetorical figures
       a,   ellipsis;
       b,   hyperbaton;
       c,   repetition;
       d,   paranomasia;
       e,   antithesis;
       f,   suspension;
       g,   epistrophe;
       h,   gradation; etc.

V.   Musical criticism

    this teaches:

    A.   The internal character of musical scales

         a,   how it happens that some sound smooth but
               others noisier;
         b,   application to the expression of various
               passions.

B.   The inner character of the musical styles

     a,   musical wit;
     b,   mood;
     c,   novelty;
     d,   the unexpected;
     e,   the extraordinary;
     f,   the wondrous;
     g,   grace;
     h,   strength;
     i,   richness;
     j,   greatness and nobility; etc.

C.   The inner character of the musical genres
     (See Musical genres under musical thetoric.)

D.   Musical taste

     a,   national taste
     b,   taste of temperament.
        <Temperamentsgeschmack>

E.   The practical execution of musical pieces

     a,   vocal;
     b,   instrumental;
     c,   both together;
     d,   with regard to place;
     e,   with regard to time.

APPENDIX II

GUIDO ADLER'S MUSICOLOGICAL SCHEMA

I. Historical (history of music according to
    epochs, peoples, kingdoms, countries,
    provinces, cities, schools of art, artists)

    A. Musical paleography (notations)

    B. Historical foundation classes
        (organization of musical forms)

    C. Historical succession of precepts

        1. as they are found in the works of
            art of each epoch
        2. as they are taught by the theorists
            of the times in question
        3. kinds of aesthetic practice

    D. History of musical instruments

Auxiliary sciences: General history with paleography,
chronology, diplomatics, bibliography, library and
archive science. Literary history and linguistics.
Liturgical history. History of the mimic arts and the
dance. Biography of composers, statistics of musical

dance. Biography of composers, statistics of musical
associations, institutions, and performances.

   II.   Systematic (arrangement of the highest precepts in
         the individual branches of musical art)

         A.   Investigating and founding of the same in

              1.   harmony (tonal or tonic)
              2.   rhythmics (temporary and temporal)
              3.   melics (coherence of tonal and temporal)

         B.   Aesthetics of the art of music

              1.   comparison and evaluation of the precepts
                   and their relation to the apperceiving
                   subject for the purpose of establishing
                   the criteria of the musically beautiful
              2.   complex of directly and indirectly
                   connected questions

         C.   Musical pedagogy and didactics (compilation of
              the precepts with regard to didactic purposes)

              1.   theory of music
              2.   theory of harmony
              3.   counterpoint
              4.   theory of composition
              5.   theory of orchestration
              6.   methods of instruction in voice and
                   instrumental playing

    D.   Musicology <u><Musikologie></u> (examination and
        comparison for ethnographic purposes)

Auxiliary sciences: Acoustics and mathematics.
Physiology (sound perception). Psychology (conception,
judgment and feeling of sound). Logic (musical
thought). Grammar (meter and poetics). Pedagogy.
Aesthetics, etc.

APPENDIX III

MUSICOLOGICAL SCHEMA GLEANED
FROM THIS CRITIQUE

I. Musical histories in general

    A. Anecdotal

    B. Scientific

        1. Those using the methods of the natural sciences
        2. Those using the methods of the human sciences

II. Lexicography

    A. Brief definition of musical terms

    B. Cover the entire field of music

    C. Biographical

    D. Bio-bibliographical

    E. Special topics, e.g., musical instruments

III. Notation

    A. Letter and cipher

    B. Neumatic

    C. Mensural

    D. Common practice

    E. 20th-century practices

IV. Organology

    A. Percussion instruments

    B. String instruments

    C. Wind instruments

    D. Electronic instruments

V. Performance practice

    A. Comparative

    B. Practical

VI.   Bibliography and textual criticism

    A.   Bibliography

        1.   Just publication data
        2.   Annotated
        3.   Union list
        4.   Bio-biography

    B.   Textual criticism

        1.   <u>Urtext</u>
        2.   Diplomatic
        3.   Critical

VII. Acoustics

    A.   Mathematical

    B.   Physical

    C.   Physiological

VIII. Aesthetics and criticism

    A.   Mimetic

        1.   Natural
        2.   Emotional

B.   Formalistic

C.   Existential

IX.   Education in music

A.   Music as an educational tool

B.   Teaching of music itself

X.   Ethnomusicology

A.   Organology

B.   Song texts

C.   Native typology and classifications

D.   Role and status of musicians in a given
culture

E.   Function of music in a given culture

F.   Music seen as a creative activity

G.   Methodological considerations

XI.   Music theory

A.   Compositional processes

    B. Practical

        1. Mathematical acoustics
        2. Humanistic-cultural
        3. Musical dialectics
        4. Physiological acoustics

    C. Speculative

XII. Auxiliary sciences

    A. Paleography

    B. Philology

    C. Chronology

    D. Archival sources

    E. Linguistics

    F. Biography

    G. Psychology and psychiatry

    H. Etc.

INDEX

Studies in The History and Interpretation of Music

1. Hugo Meynell, **The Art of Handel's Operas**

2. Dale A. Jorgenson, **Moritz Hauptmann of Leipzig**

3. Nancy van Deusen, **The Harp and the Soul: Studies in Mediaeval Music**

4. James L. Taggart, **Franz Joseph Haydn's Keyboard Sonatas: An Untapped Gold Mine**

5. William E. Grim, **The Faust Legend in Music and Literature**

6. Richard R. La Croix (ed.), **Augustine on Music: An Interdisciplinary Collection of Essays**

7. Clifford Taylor, **Musical Idea and the Design Aesthetic in Contemporary Music: A Text for Discerning Appraisal of Musical Thought in Western Culture**

8. Mary Gilbertson, **The Metaphysics of Alliteration in** *Pearl*

9. Stephen Barnes, **MUZAK—The Hidden Messages in Music: A Social Psychology of Culture**

10. Felix-Eberhard von Cube, **The Book of the Musical Artwork**, David Neumeyer (trans.)

11. Robert C. Luoma, **Music, Mode and Words in Lasso's Last Works**

12. John A. Kimmey, **A Critique of Musicology: Clarifying the Scope, Limits and Purposes of Musicology**

13. Kent A. Holliday, **Reproducing Pianos Past and Present**